Holiday Baking

Holiday Baking

new AND traditional recipes FOR wintertime holidays

BY SARA PERRY

PHOTOGRAPHS BY LEIGH BEISCH

CHRONICLE BOOKS

SAN FRANCISCO

Library of Congress Cataloging-in-Publication Data available.

ISBN 0-8118-4556-7

Manufactured in China

Design by Julia Flagg
Photo assistance by Angelica Cao
Food styling by Merilee Bordin
Food styling assistance by Lou Bustamante
Prop styling by Sara Slavin

The photographer wishes to thank the photo team, especially
Merilee Bordin for her energy and creativity in this project.

Distributed in Canada by Raincoast Books
9050 Shaughnessy Street
Vancouver, British Columbia V6P 6E5

10 9 8 7 6 5 4 3 2 1

Chronicle Books LLC
85 Second Street
San Francisco, California 94105

www.chroniclebooks.com

ACKNOWLEDGMENTS

Thanks go to the many chefs and cooks I have interviewed
over the years for *The Oregonian*'s TasteMaker column,
especially David Kobos, Ron Paul, Jan Lambert, Marilyn
DeVault, and Jeremy Karp. Also to those friends and
colleagues who generously shared their ideas, expertise,
time, and recipes, especially Amy Treadwell at Chronicle
Books, Suzi Kitman, Sharon Maasdam, Susan Friedland,
Vida Lee Mick, Wendy Smolen, Ethel Weisberg, and Selma
Paul. To Rebecca Pepper, for her editorial assistance.
To Karen Kirtley, whose editorial eye and attention to detail
are invaluable—and her recipe for Texas sheet cake is one
of the best.

And, as always, my thanks go to Bill LeBlond, editorial
director, cookbooks, at Chronicle Books, for his trust,
patience, and friendship.

To my friends and colleagues
Jane Zwinger and **Karen Brooks.**
Their help, insights, and ways around the kitchen
(and a paragraph) make me shine.

• • • • • • •

CONTENTS

● ● ● ● ● ●

8

Introduction
Time to splurge

10

Baking Tips Galore
Including successful baking steps,
the right ingredients and tools, and
baking with kids

18

THANKSGIVING
FOURTH THURSDAY IN NOVEMBER

N	O	V	E	M	B	E	R
M	T	W	TH	F	S	S
M	T	W	TH	F	S	S
M	T	W	TH	F	S	S
M	T	W	TH	F	S	S
M	T					

Pass the pumpkin
pie, count your
gingerbread blessings,
and praise the "two please"
dinner rolls

44

HANUKKAH
CYCLICAL, BASED ON THE LUNAR CALENDAR:
THE 25TH DAY OF THE
JEWISH MONTH OF KISLEV

K	I	S	L	E	V	
1	2	3	4	5	6	7
8	9	10	11	12	13	14
15	16	17	18	19	20	21
22	23	24	🌙	26	27	28
29	30	31				

Spin out the dreidel
cake, revel in rugelach,
and light up the party with
pear-apple strudel

70

CHRISTMAS
DECEMBER 25

D	E	C	E	M	B	E	R
1	2	3	4	5	6	7
8	9	10	11	12	13	14
15	16	17	18	19	20	21
22	23	24	25	26	27	28
29	30	31				

Stir up the fruitcake,
ice the cinnamon rolls,
and let the cookie
decorating begin

98

BOXING DAY
DECEMBER 26

D	E	C	E	M	B	E	R
1	2	3	4	5	6	7	
8	9	10	11	12	13	14	
15	16	17	18	19	20	21	
22	23	24	25	**26**	27	28	
29	30	31					

Delight in the day after Christmas, British style, with warm scones, shortbread, and chip-shot snacks and sweets

116

KWANZAA
DECEMBER 26 TO JANUARY 1

D	E	C	E	M	B	E	R
18	19	20	21	22	23	24	
25	**26**	**27**	**28**	**29**	**30**	**31**	
J	A	N	U	A	R	Y	
1	2	3	4	5	6	7	
8	9	10	11	12	13	14	

Honor history and the harvest with cashew caramel cracker bars, church supper carrot cake, and sweet spoonbread soufflé

140

NEW YEAR'S
DECEMBER 31 AND JANUARY 1

D	E	C	E	M	B	E	R
25	26	27	28	29	30	**31**	
J	A	N	U	A	R	Y	
1	2	3	4	5	6	7	
8	9	10	11	12	13	14	
15	16	17	18	19	20	21	

Celebrate with minutes-to-midnight meringue, a morning-after omelet, and halftime chocolate madness

Index 164

Table of Equivalents 168

INTRODUCTION
Time to Splurge

● ● ● ● ● ● ●

Here they are, the old-fashioned recipes you loved as a child, the ones that meant a holiday was here or just around the corner. And there are other recipes, too—new ones, straight from the oven, with contemporary twists stylish enough to celebrate the season with panache and tasty enough to please the child in all of us.

● ● ●

At no time of the year are traditions more alive than during the holidays, especially in the kitchen. For some bakers, it's all about going to the old recipe box to choose from among the favorites—your mother's pumpkin pie, your bubbee's apricot rugelach, and those ever-so-sweet dinner rolls your best friend never seems to make enough of. For others, it's the chance to update a classic favorite with different ingredients and time-saving methods or to try something altogether new and enticing from a different culture's holiday tradition, another family's custom, or the pages of a favorite food magazine or newspaper.

Holiday Baking is here to help you celebrate, with more than 65 recipes highlighting six wintertime holidays—Thanksgiving, Hanukkah, Christmas, Boxing Day, Kwanzaa, and New Year's. Some holidays are religious, while others are secular. Most are centuries old, though

Kwanzaa was first celebrated in 1966. All are linked with distinctive baked goods reflecting the history, the lore, and the culinary habits of the people who observe them. In this book, we explore each holiday by sampling those time-honored, oven-baked specialties.

From beloved GINGERBREAD MEN AND A FEW OF THEIR HOLIDAY FRIENDS to a peanut-buttery KWANZAA PUZZLE COOKIE to a regal BUCKINGHAM PALACE SHORTBREAD for Boxing Day, there are delectable holiday cookies too good to go missing from anyone's cookie jar. You'll find a grandmother's sweet APRICOT NOODLE KUGEL, delectable THANKSGIVING DINNER ORANGE ROLLS from an old farm journal, and SOUL-SATISFYING BISCUITS whose ancestry was never determined. Sweet treats include a four-year-old's "I can do it" dessert, my own family's favorite double-layer Christmas SNOWFLAKE CAKE, and a dynamite New Year's Eve CHOCOLATE BROWNIE TERRINE.

Baking childhood favorites with your own children and grandchildren is a way of keeping family traditions strong. Kids love the thrill—and the mess—of baking. Since they learn by touching, tasting, feeling, smelling, and listening, baking with an older relative or friend is an ideal way for them to pick up new skills and learn the stories behind the recipes. For a sweet and festive Hanukkah, preschoolers love to poke and smoosh cinnamon red hots into cored-out apples to make yummy, colorful BAKED CANDY APPLES. Before or after Santa's presents are open, older pixie Picassos can help with breakfast by creating and decorating a CINNAMON-ROLL CHRISTMAS TREE, and that's just the beginning of the season's shared adventures. In *Holiday Baking* you'll find lots of recipes specially created for baking with children.

The easy-to-follow recipes gathered here are ready to mix and match with your holiday plans as well as to satisfy every appetite from the first meal of the day through a toast to the midnight hour. When it comes to breakfast, IT'S-THANKSGIVING-MORNING-BUT-THEY-*STILL*-DESERVE-SOMETHING-SPECIAL APPLE PUFF PANCAKE, a Hanukkah STREUSEL-TOP SOUR CREAM COFFEE CAKE, and a versatile Kwanzaa SWEET SPOONBREAD SOUFFLÉ give everyone in the family a reason to start celebrating early. For a holiday gathering, homey favorites like Thanksgiving MAPLE PUMPKIN PIE or STICKY-TOP GINGERBREAD are perfect desserts to partner with a sophisticated Hanukkah PEAR-APPLE STRUDEL WITH ROSEMARY WHITE CHOCOLATE GANACHE or a divine Kwanzaa CHURCH SUPPER CARROT CAKE. Sassy

CASHEW CARAMEL CRACKER BARS, CANDY CANE CUPCAKES, OLD-AS-PILGRIMS MOLASSES CRINKLES, and PETITE FRENCH ALMOND CAKES—they're all here, and all too good to resist.

If you're a novice in the kitchen, this book will help you shine. Successful baking takes practice, like riding a bike. But the unfamiliar soon becomes second nature. The grand old recipes in the book have stood the test of time. They have been baked and tested repeatedly. In earlier generations, people had a limited repertoire of recipes they used time after time. After making a recipe fifty or sixty times, they had it figured out. Newer recipes, too, enjoy an anyone-can-do-it reputation. BACKYARD APPLE TREE CRISP and THE AMAZING LEFTOVER EGGNOG AND CINNAMON ROLL BREAD PUDDING, to name just two, give near-instant gratification.

Both new and veteran bakers will find the first chapter of *Holiday Baking* chock-full of helpful reminders. Be sure to read it. From helpful steps to essential ingredients and tools, from tips for storing, freezing, and mailing to ideas for having fun in the kitchen with kids, there is valuable information for everyone.

So thumb through these pages, get out the eggs and the butter, and build your own family traditions. May all your holidays be warm, memorable, and filled with good things to eat from your kitchen.

Baking Tips Galore

INCLUDING SUCCESSFUL BAKING STEPS, THE RIGHT INGREDIENTS AND TOOLS, AND BAKING WITH KIDS

• • • • • • •

STEPS FOR SUCCESSFUL BAKING

Following a recipe can be simple and straightforward, yet there are certain fundamental steps to follow. Easy as they may seem, they are crucial for success. The following pages describe each step and offer helpful tips to ensure that your time in the kitchen is a pleasure with no sad surprises.

1. Read over the entire recipe before you begin.

2. Have all the ingredients—and the right ingredients—in place, and make sure they are at room temperature.

3. Preheat the oven, and use an oven thermometer.

4. Choose the proper measuring tools, baking sheets, and cake pans, and have other useful kitchen tools close at hand.

5. Have baking sheets and pans at room temperature.

6. Trust your eyes, don't watch the clock, and jot down notes.

1. Read over the entire recipe before you begin.
Sure, you glanced at the ingredients, but did you read the instructions? Probably not. Make it a habit to read the directions thoroughly before you get started, so that you understand the sequence, the techniques, and the timing. Many recipes have recipes within them—for a pie's crust, a cake's frosting, or the filling and sauce for a strudel or crisp. It's up to the baker to make sure these separate components come together in the right order. Also, if you're like me and can't wait to get started, you often overlook the fact that an ingredient called for in the first paragraph of the directions, such as the sugar used for creaming with the butter, is only half the amount called for in the ingredients list. It turns out the rest is added along with the egg whites, as directed in paragraph four—whoops! I've tried to tip you off by adding the word "divided" to any ingredient used more than once. All the same, it's important to remind yourself to find out when and where each ingredient comes into play.

2. Have all the ingredients—and the right ingredients—in place, and make sure they are at room temperature.
Company is coming, the eggs are lightly beaten, and—omigosh—where is the unsweetened chocolate? We've all been there. Take a cue from professional bakers, who live by the French phrase *mise en place,* or "put into place," which is the excellent habit of setting out all the tools and measuring all the ingredients before getting started.

As you read over the recipe, make sure that you are using the ingredients called for and that they are at room temperature. Substitutions will alter the results. Using skim milk instead of whole milk affects tenderness, and margarine does not taste or act like butter. If your ingredients are straight from the refrigerator, or if they're too warm, disappointments are likely. Butter that's too cool will curdle the batter, and butter that's too warm will cause cookies to flatten like pancakes while baking. I've added "at room temperature" to items in the ingredients list that are likely to be chilled. Still, it is important to remember that *all* ingredients, unless noted, should be between 65°F and 70°F.

Here are the most elemental baking ingredients, with tips on their use, how to store them, and the best way to bring them to room temperature.

BUTTER

I use UNSALTED butter for baking because it has a sweeter, more delicate taste. (Salted butters, labeled "sweet cream," vary in the amount of salt added by the manufacturer, which makes adjusting the saltiness of your recipe difficult.) Store butter, tightly wrapped, in the refrigerator for up to 1 month or in the freezer for up to 6 months. Since butter absorbs flavors and aromas, especially if it's unsalted, be sure it is well sealed. I keep butter in its original packaging inside a sealable freezer bag.

At room temperature, a stick of butter gives slightly when pressed but still holds its shape. (If you took its temperature with an instant-read thermometer, it would be about 67°F.) In a hurry? Cut chilled butter into small pieces and leave it out at room temperature for about 15 minutes. If it is frozen, use a grater. (Using the microwave is too risky: the butter melts in the middle before softening around the edges.)

Unless otherwise noted, unsalted butter was used to test all the recipes in this book. Supermarkets now offer European-style, high-fat butters, which are tempting. But they don't make enough difference in most baked goods to justify the extra cost. There is one exception: for a plain buttercream frosting, where butter is the star, European-style butter is worth the splurge.

A NOTE ABOUT SHORTENING AND MARGARINE: Shortening, a solid vegetable oil, is often used in pie and pastry dough. Tasteless and odorless, it helps to create a flakier crust or a more solid cookie. In the 1950s, it was the popular and economical fat to use for many cookies. (Since vegetable shortening is hydrogenated and contains trans fatty acids, you may wish to use a zero trans-fat shortening, such as Spectrum Organic Shortening, Earth Balance Shortening, or Crisco Zero Trans Fat Shortening.)

If you must use margarine products instead of butter, know that oil levels vary and often affect a recipe. In most recipes, regular stick margarine can be substituted for butter in equal amounts. But with spreads, which may contain a lot of water, the results will be unpredictable. If you want butter's flavor in a recipe, you won't get it with margarine.

FLOUR

All-purpose bleached flour is most commonly used in home baking. Flour also comes unbleached. Different types of flour as well as different brands have subtle differences in flavor and texture, but overall the differences are minimal. Unless the recipe is specific, use whichever flour you prefer. CAKE FLOUR, also known as soft or southern flour, is used to create tender, fine-crumb cakes, cookies, and biscuits. Pillsbury all-purpose unbleached flour and its Softasilk cake flour were used in the recipes in *Holiday Baking*.

To measure flour accurately, first stir, then spoon the loose flour into the cup until it is piled high. Use the straight side of a metal spatula or knife to level off excess flour. Do not use the measuring cup as a scoop, and do not tap or press the flour into the cup. For best results and flavor, purchase flour in the amount you are likely to use within 6 months and store it in an airtight container at room temperature. (If the temperature gets above 70°F, you're inviting bugs.)

SUGAR

GRANULATED SUGAR is most commonly used in baking. BAKER'S or SUPERFINE SUGAR is occasionally used in a recipe or as a topping when a more delicate texture is desired. Superfine sugar is available in most supermarket baking sections. To make your own, you can use a processor or blender to process granulated sugar in small batches for about 20 seconds.

POWDERED or CONFECTIONER'S SUGAR is commonly used for dusting baked cookies and cakes and for making frostings. The fine-grained sugar is mixed with small amounts of cornstarch to keep it from clumping.

BROWN SUGARS (light or dark), which are granulated sugars enhanced with molasses, are measured by packing them firmly into the measuring cup. Make sure brown sugars are stored in airtight containers or thick plastic bags to prevent hardening. To soften hardened or lumpy sugar, add an apple wedge to the bag, seal, and leave it overnight. (Don't forget to remove the apple in the morning.) Alternatively, you can use the microwave to soften hardened sugar by placing a lettuce leaf on top of the sugar in a covered container and heating for 30 to 60 seconds. The recipes in this book were tested with C&H pure cane sugar (granulated, golden brown, dark brown, powdered, and baker's).

SALT

Salt brightens any recipe and helps bring out the flavors. Many types of salt are available, from the coarse kosher variety to artisan sea salts. But ordinary TABLE SALT is best to use when baking because its small, uniform grains flow freely and blend easily with flour and other dry ingredients.

A FINAL NOTE ON DRY INGREDIENTS: Store dry ingredients in a cool, dry environment, and keep them in your pantry for no longer than 6 months. Over time, spices and herbs lose their strength and flavor, and the leavening agents in baking powder become less effective. When you make a purchase, check to see if there is a "sell by" date and go for the farthest date out. To keep track when you get home, add the current date to the label with a permanent marker.

EGGS

Use grade AA large eggs for the recipes in this book, and use the freshest eggs possible. (Check the "sell by" date on the side of the carton.) Once you bring the eggs home, refrigerate them in their carton, not in your refrigerator's egg tray. To bring them to room temperature, take them out of the refrigerator 1 hour before using, or place them in warm water and let them sit for about 5 minutes.

When a recipe calls for separated eggs, separate the yolks from the whites when the eggs are cold, then let them reach room temperature. EGG WHITES whip best and gain the most volume when they are whisked at room temperature or slightly warmer. Also, be sure your utensils are squeaky clean and without a hint of grease.

DAIRY

WHOLE (3.5 percent fat) or LOW-FAT (2 percent) MILK was used to prepare the recipes in this book. FAT-FREE or SKIM

MILK, with less than 1 percent fat, will alter the texture of baked goods. When a recipe calls for cream, I use HEAVY (WHIPPING) CREAM (36 to 40 percent fat), not whipping cream (30 to 36 percent). Many supermarkets now carry ultra-pasteurized milks and creams, which have been processed for a longer shelf life. I prefer to use pasteurized milk whenever possible.

3. Preheat the oven, and use an oven thermometer.

It takes 15 minutes to preheat an oven's interior to a desired and uniform temperature. Regardless of the quality of the oven, it loses its initial factory temperature calibrations over time. Since temperature is critical to the outcome of any baked good, it's wise to invest in an inexpensive oven thermometer to check your oven's temperature for accuracy. To test the recipes in this book, I used the Taylor Classic Oven Guide Thermometer (about $15), and I discovered that my oven was off by about 10 degrees.

4. Choose the proper measuring tools, baking sheets, and cake pans, and have other useful kitchen tools close at hand.

MEASURING CUPS AND SPOONS

There are two different types of measuring containers: dry and liquid. DRY MEASURING CUPS come in nested sets and are usually made of metal or plastic. They measure in terms of cups or portions of cups. I prefer stainless steel cups with straight rims because they are sturdy and easy to level with a straight-edged implement. LIQUID MEASURING CUPS have spouts and graduated markers. Usually they measure in terms of cups and ounces. LIQUID GRADUATED BEAKERS are also available. When measuring a liquid, set the cup or beaker on a level surface and let the liquid rest before reading the gauge. I own 1-cup, 2-cup, 4-cup, and 8-cup Pyrex glass measuring cups and often use the larger ones

as mixing bowls. I also use two nifty 1- and 2-cup angled measuring cups made by Oxo that allow you to read measurements from above, as well as a plastic Emsa beaker with six different measuring scales. For accuracy, use the smallest cup size that holds the amount of liquid you need.

MEASURING SPOONS are used to measure very small quantities of liquid and dry ingredients. They come in nested sets, usually connected by a ring. The best are stainless steel with straight rims. While round spoons are most common, they also come in elongated shapes for easier entry into the narrow openings of spice jars.

A FINAL NOTE: It's a good idea to verify that your measuring cups and spoons are properly calibrated by checking their capacity against a second set of measuring tools. Make sure that the ½-cup mark and the 1 teaspoon measure actually yield ½ cup and 1 teaspoon.

BAKING SHEETS AND CAKE PANS

The best BAKING or COOKIE SHEETS are shiny and heavy gauge, with no sides or with two slightly turned up sides. Thin sheets warp easily, and dark ones can cause cookies to overbrown. It's a good idea to have two or three baking sheets at hand. I have two medium (10-by-13-inch) and two large (14-by-16-inch) baking sheets, so that when I'm baking cookies, while one is in the oven and one is cooling, I can assemble the next set of cookies on the others. A JELLY ROLL or SHEET PAN resembles a cookie sheet but has four sides to contain batter. It's used for making pinwheel cakes, roulades, and certain bar cookies, and it's also great for corraling nuts while they're toasting in the oven.

CAKE PANS come in a variety of sizes, but most recipes call for either 8-inch or 9-inch round pans. Light-colored aluminum pans are preferable, since they conduct heat evenly and quickly. A SPRINGFORM PAN is round, high, and straight sided, with a spring-loaded hinge to release the sides of the pan from the base. This allows delicate baked goods such as cheesecakes to be removed easily. It's important to make sure the seal is tight and snug so that the springform pan doesn't leak. SQUARE and RECTANGULAR CAKE or BAKING PANS are handy for brownies and other bar cookies. Choose light-colored metal or aluminum pans with 2-inch-high sides. Glass baking dishes are useful for fruit crisps and crumbles.

The recipes in *Holiday Baking* have been tested with the size and type of pan they call for. If you have to make a substitution, be sure the pan you use is the same volume as the one specified, and be aware that you may need to adjust the baking time. You can check a pan's volume by measuring the amount of water it takes to fill it. (Also see "Have baking sheets and pans at room temperature," facing page.)

SOME HANDY KITCHEN TOOLS
Glance down any store's kitchenware aisle, and you'll be convinced that a tool exists for every purpose, and then some. Beyond the basics such as bowls, mixers, sifters, sieves, saucepans, rolling pins, wire whisks, wooden spoons, and cooling racks, there are specialty items designed for a specific task or simply to catch your fancy. It's a good idea to have a pastry brush. But do you need a pastry crimper wheel for sealing and decorating the edges of a piecrust? I prefer to use my fingers.

For good, sound advice on what you need in the way of kitchen tools and equipment, check out the detailed guidelines and suggestions in Regan Daley's *In the Sweet Kitchen* (Artisan Books, 2001) or in *Baking Illustrated,* from the editors of *Cook's Illustrated* magazine (America's Test Kitchen, 2004). The following is my list of the five special tools I couldn't live without. Other bakers have their own favorites. If you don't already have yours, you'll soon find your one-and-onlys.

HANDS: Those two very handy items have fingers attached. They're always with you and can tell you with your eyes shut if the dough is too sticky or as soft as a baby's bottom. Hands are the ultimate kitchen tool and gadget. They are sensitive and marvelous at forming cookies, kneading dough, and letting you know with a touch when something is too hot, too cold, or just right. Use them whenever you can.

PARCHMENT PAPER: This is the best friend of the tidy baker (and the messy one too). Treated with silicone, the paper is nonstick and grease resistant. It prevents baked goods from attaching to baking sheets and cake pans, and it makes a handy sling for removing bar cookies from the pan. A sheet of parchment paper under a mixing bowl keeps counters clean and provides a resting place for batter-coated spoons and spatulas. The paper can also act as a funnel and a landing spot for sifted ingredients. Like waxed paper, it is available in rolls in the baking section of most supermarkets. It also comes in bulk, precut sheets at retail baking-supply stores. One box containing a thousand 16⅜-inch-by-24-inch sheets costs about $38 and lasts for years. (Parchment paper also makes great holiday wrapping paper.)

PORTABLE TIMER (ON A STRING OR WITH A CLIP): Hickory, dickory, dock, the mouse ran up the clock. The clock struck one, and the cake was done, and I was out watering the flowers. When you're baking, carry a portable timer wherever you go.

HEATPROOF SILICONE SPATULA: Everyone is familiar with rubber spatulas, those flat, flexible devices many of us use as if they were wooden spoons. They are good to the last drop for getting all the batter and all the buttercream out of the mixing bowl. The only trouble is they tend to melt under high heat or to fleck off bits of rubber as they harden with age. The new silicone spatulas retain their shape under high heat and keep their pliability with use and age.

MICROPLANE GRATER: I admit it. I used to avoid zesting—separating the colored part of the citrus peel, with its highly flavored oils, from the bitter white pith—because I never found a grater I liked. My little zester, with its row of tiny holes, yielded fine threads instead of finely minced peel. The Microplane grater, which looks like a woodworker's rasp, is a tool that does it all, from zesting citrus to shaving off soft flakes of hard chocolate and fresh ginger.

AND ONE MORE: My handy-dandy 12-inch METAL RULER. I don't know where it came from—maybe an art class in college?—but I couldn't live without it in the kitchen. I use it for everything from a straightedge swipe across a flour-heaped measuring cup, to calculating how thin I really did roll the cookie dough, to filling in as a bookmark when I'm going from the cakes to the frostings. It's a trouper.

5. **Have baking sheets and pans at room temperature.**
After that first batch of cookies, your baking sheet will no longer be at room temperature. If you place dough on it, the hot sheet will melt the dough, causing the cookies to run and to bake improperly. To avoid this, have extra baking sheets on hand, or run room-temperature water over the underside of the baking sheet to cool it between batches. It's best to bake cookies one sheet at a time, in the center of the oven. For cookies (or any baked good) to bake and brown evenly, the oven's hot air should circulate freely around them. This doesn't happen when the baking sheets are stacked on shelves, one above the other, or when you use a jelly roll pan instead of a baking sheet. If you're rushed and need to bake two sheets at once, rotate them from front to back and top to bottom halfway through the baking sequence.

6. **Trust your eyes, don't watch the clock, and jot down notes.**
In this book's recipes, certain steps are described with visual cues as well as approximate times: "Bake until the muffins have risen, are lightly browned, and a toothpick inserted in the middle comes out clean, about 25 minutes."

It is important to understand that mixing and baking times are always approximate because they depend on many factors, from an individual's skills to an oven's accuracy. Use suggested times only as guidelines, and place your faith mainly in other signs of doneness, your intuition, and what you see with your eyes. Use indicators of doneness, such as a golden brown top, a crisp crust, or a top that "springs back when lightly touched," to develop your own vocabulary of visual cues, and when you find a discrepancy, be sure to jot it down in the recipe's margin for the next time. My cookbooks are my collective kitchen diary, with notes, comments, and even dates scribbled in the margins.

TIPS FOR STORING

While fresh is always best and most baked goods taste their finest straight from the oven or within a few hours, at times it's a wonderful lift to have extra treats stashed away. In this section you'll find suggestions for storing and freezing holiday baked goods for the next time friends visit unexpectedly or a craving for warm-from-the-oven cookies suddenly strikes.

First and foremost, if any baked good contains a perishable ingredient such as cream or custard, store it in the refrigerator, and for no longer than 3 days.

Cookies

Once cookies are completely cool, they can be stored in an airtight tin or plastic container. Unless otherwise noted in the recipe, most cookies keep their flavor and texture at room temperature for 3 to 5 days. To keep decorated cookies looking good, let the frosting set, then layer them between sheets of waxed or parchment paper. If you are storing more than one type of cookie, keep them separate. If you mix soft cookies with crisp ones, the crisp ones will soften too. If you've been looking forward to using your Frosty the Snowman cookie jar over the holidays, you might consider lining it with a resealable plastic bag for airtight storage, although this is probably unnecessary, since your cookies will be gone in a flash.

Cookie dough can be refrigerated, if wrapped, for 2 to 3 days. Since raw dough freezes well, it is handy to make some ahead to bake up during the busy holidays or to give as gifts. When preparing dough for freezing, be sure to shape it in a form that will be convenient to use once it thaws. Tightly wrap the dough in plastic wrap, then wrap it in foil or put it in a resealable freezer bag. Don't forget to add a label with the date and contents (and with instructions, if it's to be a gift). Raw dough will keep for up to 6 months in the freezer. Before using, thaw it, wrapped, in the refrigerator.

Freeze unbaked, cut-out cookies on a cookie sheet. After the cookies freeze, layer them between parchment or waxed paper in a sealable freezer container and refreeze. Most cookies can be transferred straight from the freezer to the baking sheet, although the baking time will be longer and you'll need to use the visual cues for doneness. You can also let the cookies thaw, covered, before baking. As a rule, decorated cookies don't freeze well because the frosting tends to separate from the cookies.

A NOTE ON MAILING COOKIES: If you plan to mail a taste of the holidays, choose sturdy cookies with simple shapes, such as OLD-AS-PILGRIMS MOLASSES CRINKLES (page 22), RETRO RAISIN CRISSCROSS COOKIES (page 24), or CASHEW CARAMEL CRACKER BARS (page 125). Wrap the cookies in pairs, back to back, in plastic wrap, and place them flat or on end in a tin, a box, or any other durable decorative container. Once the container is full, pad the top with crushed parchment or waxed paper to prevent the cookies from shaking and breaking. Place the container in a heavy-duty box, surrounding the cookie container on all sides with shredded paper, plastic bubble wrap, or other light packing filler. Seal, label, and mark the box "perishable."

Cakes, Pies, and Other Goodies

CAKES with whipped cream or custard and cheesecakes should always be stored in the refrigerator. To store a frosted cake that does not require refrigeration, it's best to use a cake dome or a covered cake carrier. If you don't have one, be inventive. Invert a large bowl over the cake, or stick toothpicks in the top and sides, drape plastic wrap over the toothpicks, and seal the wrap underneath the plate. To store a plain or layer cake, even overnight, wrap each layer individually in plastic wrap and then in foil as soon as it is completely cool. If you want to freeze it, place the wrapped cake inside a resealable plastic bag. It is best to freeze unfrosted cakes for no longer than 2 to 3 months. To thaw a plain cake, leave it wrapped at room temperature.

It's risky to freeze a frosted cake, since there is a chance the frosting will turn the cake soggy, take on moisture while thawing, or separate from the cake. If you must, place the frosted cake in the freezer to harden the frosting before placing the cake in a container to prevent crushing. To thaw, leave it covered at room temperature for 2 to 3 hours, and hope for a good result. A frozen layer cake will thaw in about 1 hour, and cupcakes in about 30 minutes.

If you plan on storing a PIE, cool it thoroughly and use a cake dome or covered cake carrier. Custard pies, including pumpkin, should always be stored in the refrigerator, for no longer than 3 days. This is also true for fruit tarts and crisps. Pies with meringue are best eaten within several hours. While they can be stored, chilled, for 1 or 2 days, I don't recommend it. The meringue begins to break down, and the pie's flavor and texture change. In general, I avoid freezing homemade pies. All that work, and then the crust gets soggy once it thaws.

BISCUITS, SCONES, and MUFFINS are meant to be eaten fresh. Period. In a matter of hours they begin to taste stale. If you have leftovers you would like to keep until the next day, store them in an airtight container. To serve them, microwave on high for about 20 seconds, or wrap loosely in foil and set in a preheated 350°F oven for 10 minutes, and serve with plenty of butter and jam.

TIPS FOR BAKING WITH KIDS

The scents and sensations of baking as a child linger for a lifetime. For a parent, relative, or adult friend, the experience of holiday baking is a memorable gift for a child. This book has many recipes you'll find ideal for creating together. Thumb through its pages and discover what sounds good to you both, then go over the following tips.

1. **Make sure everyone washes his or her hands with soap and water.** (Did you know that doctors and nurses scrub their hands for a full 15 seconds to make sure they're clean?) **A sneeze or a cough? It's time to wash those hands again.**

2. **Tie long hair back so it won't cloud vision or fall into the food.**

3. **Store sharp knives and cooking tools in a safe place until they are needed. Wash knives, graters, and peelers separately. If they are all thrown together in soapy water, someone might reach in and get cut.**

4. **Have oven mitts handy to remove a hot dish from the oven or the microwave.**

5. **Don't set pots on the stovetop with the handles sticking out where kids—and adults—can easily bump into them.**

6. **Have fun, use good judgment in assigning tasks, and stay close by to lend an extra hand and to offer lots of encouragement.**

The first Thanksgiving took place in the autumn of 1621, when the Pilgrims and Native Americans came together to share their harvests in what is now Plymouth, Massachusetts. Fast-forward to the 1860s, when Sarah Hale, editor of the *Boston Ladies' Magazine,* campaigned for an annual day set aside for Americans to reflect upon their heritage and their good fortune. In 1863, President Abraham Lincoln proclaimed the last Thursday in November a national holiday for giving thanks.

NOVEMBER

M	T	W	TH	F	S	S
M	T	W	TH	F	S	S
M	T	W	TH	F	S	S
M	T	W	TH	F	S	S
M	T					

Thus began a ritual Americans continue to love and respect—our official day of Thanksgiving. (In Canada, the harvest season falls earlier than in the United States, so Canadians celebrate their Thanksgiving on the second Monday in October.)

What could be more natural than to celebrate abundant blessings with an abundance of food? And so we gather our families and friends around the Thanksgiving table for a feast, thankful for one another and for our bountiful homeland.

THANKSGIVING

FOURTH THURSDAY IN NOVEMBER

• • • • • •

Cut-Out Ginger Gobblers 20

Old-as-Pilgrims Molasses Crinkles 22
Grandmother's Grown-Up Glaze 23

Retro Raisin Crisscross Cookies 24
Golden Raisin Crisscross Cookies 24
Autumn's Best Crisscross Cookies 24

Blessed Be Breakfast Quiche 25

Crunchy-Topped Blueberry Muffins 28

It's-Thanksgiving-Morning-but-They-*Still*-Deserve
Something-Special Apple Puff Pancake 30
It's-Nighttime-and-They're-*Still*-Hungry
Apple Pastry with Calvados and Golden Raisins 31

"Two Please" Thanksgiving Dinner Orange Rolls 32

Vida Lee's Maple Pumpkin Pie 35

Rustic Dried Fruit Tart 37
Cardamom Custard Sauce 39

The Ultimate Dinner Guest's Gingerbread 40
Sticky-Top Gingerbread 41
Chocolate Chip Gingerbread Cupcakes 41

Backyard Apple Tree Crisp 43

Excitement is in the air. Soon the Thanksgiving table will groan with traditional dishes that celebrate earth's bounty. It's fun to find a few surprises, too—like a plate piled high with ginger gobblers. Cut with a classic cookie cutter from golden dough rich with familiar spices and maple syrup, these tasty Toms are inspired by their spicy cousins, the gingerbread men.

For a touch of color and taste, feel free to gussy up your gobblers with ERNA NEUMAN'S ICING (page 47) once they have cooled.

MAKES ABOUT 3 DOZEN 3- TO 3½-INCH COOKIES

Cut-Out Ginger Gobblers

2 ¼ cups sifted **all-purpose flour**

½ teaspoon **baking soda**

½ teaspoon **salt**

1½ teaspoons **ground ginger**

1 teaspoon **ground allspice**

½ teaspoon **ground cinnamon**

½ cup **unsalted butter,** at room temperature

½ cup firmly packed **light brown sugar**

½ cup **maple syrup**

2 tablespoons **orange** or **apple juice** or **water**

1 teaspoon grated **lemon zest**

1. Into a medium bowl, sift together the flour, baking soda, salt, ginger, allspice, and cinnamon, then lightly whisk and set aside.

2. In a stand mixer set on medium speed, beat the butter until creamy, about 30 seconds. On medium speed, beat in the brown sugar until light and lump free. Beat in the maple syrup, orange juice, and lemon zest until blended, scraping down the sides and bottom of the bowl as necessary. Turn off the mixer, add half the flour mixture, and beat on low speed until blended. Add the remaining flour and beat until blended. Gather the dough into a 6- to 8-inch disk and wrap loosely in plastic wrap. Using a rolling pin, flatten the disk so the plastic wrap is tight and the dough is even. (This helps reduce the chilling time and makes the dough easier to roll out.) Chill for 2 hours, or until firm.

3. Preheat the oven to 350°F. Line a baking sheet with parchment paper or grease it lightly and set aside.

4. Remove the dough from the refrigerator and, if needed, soften slightly for easier handling. Roll it out ⅛ inch thick on a lightly floured board, between 2 sheets of parchment paper or heavy-duty plastic wrap, or on a pastry cloth with a cloth-covered rolling pin.

5. Lightly dip a 3- to 3½-inch turkey-shaped or Thanksgiving-themed cookie cutter in flour, then firmly press it straight down into the dough. Repeat, cutting the cookies close together to avoid rerolling. Using a spatula, carefully transfer the cookies to the baking sheet. If a cookie is to be used as an ornament, press a hole through the top with a drinking straw or large skewer.

6. Bake until the cookies are lightly browned, 10 to 12 minutes. Let the cookies firm and cool slightly on the baking sheet before transferring to a rack to cool completely.

At Thanksgiving time, my grandmother always had a big red tin filled with these crackly-topped favorites. My mom loved them too, and she made them year round. She liked to bake her cookies a few minutes longer than Nanny, giving them a crunchier texture just right for dunking in a cold glass of milk.

Over the years the spice mix has changed from Nanny's recipe to my mom's, and now to mine. Nanny's mix was equal parts ground ginger, cinnamon, and cloves; Mom used more cinnamon and ginger; and I like lots of ginger as well as a bit of white pepper for a little zing at the end of each bite. My mother and grandmother made their cookies with shortening, but I often use butter. Do as you please when it comes to the spices, the shortening, and the baking time. You can't go wrong with these family cookies. If you want to dress them up for a grown-up occasion, bake them, then add a fancy Grand Marnier glaze (see the variation at the end of the recipe).

MAKES ABOUT 3 DOZEN COOKIES

Old-as-Pilgrims Molasses Crinkles

2½ cups **all-purpose flour**

2 teaspoons **baking soda**

¼ teaspoon **salt**

2 teaspoons **ground ginger**

1 teaspoon **ground cinnamon**

½ teaspoon **ground cloves**

1 teaspoon **ground white pepper** (optional)

1. Into a medium bowl, sift the flour, baking soda, salt, ginger, cinnamon, cloves, and white pepper, if desired, then lightly whisk and set aside.

2. In a stand mixer or with a hand mixer set on low speed, beat the shortening until creamy, about 30 seconds. On medium speed, beat in the brown sugar until smooth and lump free. Beat in the egg until well blended, scraping down the sides and bottom of the bowl as necessary. Beat in the molasses and vanilla until blended. Turn off the mixer, add half the flour mixture, and beat on low speed until blended. Add the remaining flour, and beat until blended. Scrape down the dough, cover the bowl with plastic wrap, and chill for at least 1 hour.

1 cup **vegetable shortening**

1 cup firmly packed **dark** or **light brown sugar**

1 **egg,** at room temperature

¼ cup **dark** or **light molasses**

1 teaspoon **vanilla extract**

⅓ cup **granulated sugar**

Water for sprinkling

3. Preheat the oven to 375°F. Line a baking sheet with parchment paper or leave ungreased. Remove the dough from the refrigerator and, if needed, soften slightly for easier handling. Place the granulated sugar in a small bowl.

4. Using a tablespoon measure, scoop out some dough and roll it between your hands to form a 1½-inch ball (if the dough sticks to your hands, keep a bowl of cold water nearby and occasionally dip your hands in, shaking off the excess). Drop the ball into the sugar, roll to coat, and place on the baking sheet. Repeat with the remaining batter, placing the cookies 2 inches apart. Sprinkle or mist each cookie with water.

5. Bake until the tops are firm when lightly touched, about 10 minutes. For a crunchier cookie, bake for about 12 minutes. Let the cookies firm and cool slightly on the baking sheet before transferring to a rack to cool completely.

• • •

VARIATION

For Grandmother's Grown-Up Glaze, while the cookies cool slightly but are still warm on the baking sheet, whisk together 1 cup powdered sugar with 3 to 4 tablespoons Grand Marnier or another orange-flavored liqueur. Dip a spoon into the glaze and drizzle it over the warm cookies. Transfer to a rack and allow the glaze to set before serving.

In the fifties and sixties, these lemony cookies, plump with raisins, were among my mother's favorites to fix for holiday get-togethers. My brother and I would join in to help roll the dough into balls and then use forks to make that familiar crisscross pattern. Nowadays I make these cookies all the time, since they're great for snacking and sturdy enough for a sack lunch.

MAKES ABOUT 2 DOZEN COOKIES

Retro Raisin Crisscross Cookies

1 ¾ cups **all-purpose flour**

¾ teaspoon **cream of tartar**

¾ teaspoon **baking soda**

¼ teaspoon **salt**

½ cup **unsalted butter,** at room temperature

¾ cup **granulated sugar**

1 **egg,** at room temperature

½ teaspoon **pure lemon extract**

½ teaspoon **grated lemon zest**

1 cup **raisins**

1. Preheat the oven to 350°F. Line a baking sheet with parchment paper or leave ungreased and set aside.

2. Into a medium bowl, sift together the flour, cream of tartar, baking soda, and salt, then lightly whisk and set aside.

3. In a stand mixer or with a hand mixer set on low speed, beat the butter until creamy, about 30 seconds. On medium speed, add the sugar and beat until light and fluffy. Beat in the egg, lemon extract, and zest until well blended, scraping down the sides and bottom of the bowl as necessary. Turn off the mixer, add half of the flour mixture, and beat on low speed until blended. Add the remaining flour and beat until blended. The dough will be stiff. Stir in the raisins. Chill the dough for one hour.

4. Pinch off a tablespoonful of the dough at a time, and roll each into a ball. Arrange on the baking sheet, 2 ½ inches apart. Lightly dip the back of a fork into flour and flatten the cookies with the tines to make ridges, first in one direction, then the other. Bake until the tops are golden, 12 to 16 minutes. Transfer the cookies to a rack to cool.

• • •

VARIATIONS

For Golden Raisin Crisscross Cookies, follow the main recipe, substituting **golden raisins** for the black ones. For Autumn's Best Crisscross Cookies, substitute **chopped dried fruit** for the raisins.

Thanks to this simple quiche, you can count your blessings over a tasty morning meal on the day of the Thanksgiving feast. An irresistible interpretation of the simple quiche Lorraine, it includes plenty of bacon and the best of the Swiss cheeses, Emmentaler or Gruyère.

To simplify your life, stash a couple of frozen piecrusts in your freezer. If you need to create a last-minute quiche straight from the refrigerator, simply keep the egg and milk amounts the same and use what you have on hand to make spur-of-the-moment fillings. You can vary the type of cheese you use and add cubed ham, crumbled sausage, sliced mushrooms, or anything you and your guests might enjoy in an omelet or frittata.

MAKES ONE 9-INCH QUICHE, SERVING 6

Blessed Be Breakfast Quiche

FLAKY PASTRY CRUST

1¼ cups **all-purpose flour**

½ teaspoon **salt**

5 tablespoons cold **unsalted butter,** cut into small pieces

2 tablespoons cold **vegetable shortening,** cut into small pieces

4 to 6 tablespoons **ice water**

continued

1. TO MAKE THE CRUST: In a medium bowl, whisk together the flour and salt. Add the butter and shortening. Using your fingers or a pastry blender, work the butter and shortening into the flour mixture until crumbly and some pea-size pieces of fat remain. If time permits, chill the flour mixture for 30 minutes.

2. Drizzle the ice water over the flour mixture, 1 tablespoon at a time, mixing until all the flour is moistened and the pastry just clears the side of the bowl (adding an additional 1 to 2 teaspoons water if needed). Using lightly floured hands, gather the dough into a ball. Shape into a disk, wrap in plastic wrap, and chill for 1 hour.

3. Remove the dough from the refrigerator and, if needed, soften slightly for easier handling. Roll the dough out to a 12-inch circle on a lightly floured board, between 2 sheets of parchment paper or heavy-duty plastic wrap, or on a pastry cloth with a cloth-covered rolling pin. Transfer the dough to a 9-inch pie pan, easing it into the pan. Trim the overhanging edge of the pastry along the pan's edge. Chill for 30 minutes to 1 hour.

continued

Blessed Be Breakfast Quiche *continued*

FILLING

6 slices **bacon** (6 ounces uncooked), cut crosswise into 1-inch pieces

6 **eggs**

1½ cups **half-and-half**

Salt and freshly **ground black pepper**

2 cups (8 ounces) grated **Swiss Emmentaler** or **Gruyère cheese**

Large pinch of **ground nutmeg,** preferably freshly ground

4. Meanwhile, preheat the oven to 375°F.

5. Prick the bottom of the crust with a fork, line with aluminum foil, and fill to the top with pie weights or dried beans. Bake in the center of the oven until the edges begin to turn golden, about 15 minutes. Remove the weights and foil and bake until the crust is golden, 8 to 10 minutes. Remove from the oven and transfer to a rack to cool.

6. TO MAKE THE FILLING: In a medium, heavy skillet, cook the bacon pieces over medium heat, turning as needed, until brown but not crisp. Using a slotted spoon, transfer to a paper towel to drain.

7. In a medium bowl, whisk together the eggs and half-and-half until blended. Stir in the salt and pepper to taste.

8. Place the prepared piecrust on a baking sheet. Sprinkle the bottom of the crust with the bacon and cheese. Pour the egg mixture into the crust. There may be extra custard. Sprinkle the top with the nutmeg. Carefully place the quiche in the oven, and bake until the top is puffed and golden and the eggs are set, about 35 minutes (the time may vary if you are using a purchased piecrust). Transfer to a rack to cool slightly, 5 to 7 minutes. Serve warm or at room temperature.

Crunchy, crusty, and packed with blueberries, these scrumptious muffins are moist and tender. You can serve them straight from the oven in the morning, tuck them into the Thanksgiving dinner breadbasket, or enjoy them with late-night leftovers. Whenever you serve them, they'll disappear in a wink.

MAKES 12 MUFFINS

Crunchy-Topped Blueberry Muffins

TOPPING

¼ cup **all-purpose flour**

¼ cup plus 2 tablespoons **granulated sugar**

½ teaspoon **ground cinnamon**

3 tablespoons cold **unsalted butter,** cut into small pieces

MUFFINS

2 cups **all-purpose flour**

2 teaspoons **baking powder**

½ teaspoon **salt**

1 **egg,** at room temperature

⅔ cup **granulated sugar**

6 tablespoons **unsalted butter,** melted and cooled

1 cup **sour cream**

1 teaspoon **pure vanilla extract**

1 cup frozen **blueberries**

1. Preheat the oven to 375°F. Lightly grease 12 standard muffin cups with cooking spray or line with cupcake liners and set aside.

2. TO MAKE THE TOPPING: In a small bowl, whisk together the flour, sugar, and cinnamon until blended. Using your fingers or a pastry blender, work the butter into the flour mixture until the topping is crumbly. Set aside.

3. TO MAKE THE MUFFINS: In a large bowl, whisk together the flour, baking powder, and salt until well blended.

4. In a medium bowl, whisk together the egg and sugar until light. Whisk in the butter, then the sour cream and vanilla until blended. Pour the egg mixture over the flour mixture, stirring until just combined. Do not overbeat the sticky dough. Fold in the berries.

5. Spoon the batter into the prepared muffin tin. Top each muffin with about 1 tablespoon of the topping.

6. Bake until the muffins have risen and are lightly browned, and a toothpick inserted in the middle comes out clean, about 25 minutes. Do not overbake. Cool the muffins in the tin for 5 minutes, then transfer to a rack to cool slightly; otherwise, you could burn your mouth on the hot berries and the crust could separate from the muffin. (If you are not using liners, the curved blade of a grapefruit knife will help unmold the warm muffins.) The muffins are best eaten warm or within a few hours of baking.

Some call this heavenly dish an apple pancake, while others insist it's an apple flan, tart, or puffy fruit pie. In French country kitchens it's a *clafouti*. Whatever you call it, it's simple and delicious. This dish is easy as well as festive, so it's an excellent choice for breakfast on a day that's bound to be busy.

SERVES 6 TO 8

It's·Thanksgiving·Morning·but·They·*Still*·Deserve·Something·Special
Apple Puff Pancake

2 teaspoons **unsalted butter**

¾ cup **granulated sugar,** divided

½ teaspoon **ground cinnamon**

Pinch of **ground nutmeg**

4 medium to large **Granny Smith apples,** peeled, cored, and cut into ¼-inch slices

1 cup **all-purpose flour**

1½ teaspoons **baking powder**

¼ teaspoon **salt**

2 **eggs,** at room temperature

1 cup **whole milk,** at room temperature

Powdered sugar for dusting

1. Preheat the oven to 400°F. Grease a heavy, 10-inch ovenproof or cast-iron skillet with the butter and set aside.

2. In a medium bowl, mix 2 tablespoons of the sugar with the cinnamon and nutmeg. Add the apples and toss to coat. Transfer the apples to the skillet and set aside. Portions of the apples may be higher than the side of the skillet.

3. In another medium bowl, whisk together the flour, the remaining ½ cup plus 2 tablespoons sugar, baking powder, and salt until blended. In a small bowl, lightly whisk the eggs, then add the milk and whisk until blended. Whisk the egg mixture into the flour mixture until blended and smooth.

4. Pour the batter over the apples. Using the skillet's handle, give the skillet an easy back-and-forth shake to settle the ingredients. If you wish, you can level the top with a spatula. Some apples will remain only partially submerged.

5. Bake until the batter is golden, the protruding apples are tinged and golden, and a toothpick inserted in the center comes out clean, 35 to 45 minutes. Transfer to a rack to cool for 10 minutes. Dust with powdered sugar, cut into 6 to 8 wedges, and serve.

• • •

VARIATION

For an elegant last-minute dessert any time of the year, try It's-Nighttime-and-They're-*Still*-Hungry Apple Pastry with Calvados and Golden Raisins. In a cup or small bowl, combine ½ cup **golden raisins** and 2 tablespoons **Calvados** or **applejack brandy.** Microwave for 25 seconds and let the raisins soften for 15 minutes. Follow the main recipe, sprinkling the raisins and Calvados over the apples in the skillet, then proceed as directed. Accompany with slightly softened vanilla ice cream, unsweetened whipped cream, or a slice of aged white Cheddar cheese.

These golden, sweet dinner rolls are the creation of Sharon Maasdam, a home economist on the staff of the *Oregonian* known for her wonderful homemade breads. She adapted the recipe from an old *Farm Journal* cookbook more than 25 years ago. Now her family tells her it wouldn't be Thanksgiving without them. My family is picking up the tradition she graciously shared. On Thanksgiving Day, we thank goodness for Sharon.

I love the simplicity of the recipe, but mostly I adore the orange zest filling that swirls, jelly roll style, through each roll. If your plans include a large get-together, you can easily double this recipe.

MAKES ABOUT 16 ROLLS

"Two Please" Thanksgiving Dinner Orange Rolls

ROLLS

6 tablespoons **whole milk**

¼ cup **unsalted butter**

¼ cup **granulated sugar**

½ teaspoon **salt**

2 to 2¼ teaspoons (1 package) **active dry yeast**

¼ cup **warm water** (110°F to 115°F)

2 to 2¼ cups **all-purpose** or **bread flour,** divided

1 **egg,** at room temperature

1. TO MAKE THE ROLLS: In a small saucepan over medium heat, warm the milk and add the butter, sugar, and salt, stirring until the butter has melted. Transfer to the large bowl of a stand mixer and set aside to cool to lukewarm.

2. In a small bowl, sprinkle the yeast over the warm water, stir to combine, and set aside.

3. Add ¾ cup flour to the milk mixture and mix on low speed until blended, about 1 minute. Beat in the egg on medium speed until well blended, scraping down the sides and bottom of the bowl as necessary. Beat in the yeast mixture until well blended. Gradually stir in enough of the remaining flour, a little at a time, to make a soft dough that leaves the sides of the bowl.

4. Turn the dough out onto a lightly floured work surface (or use the dough hook on your mixer) and knead until smooth, satiny, and no longer sticky, 5 to 8 minutes. Transfer the dough to a lightly greased bowl and turn the dough to grease the top. Cover the bowl with plastic wrap and let the dough rise in a warm place until doubled in size, about 1 hour. Once doubled, press down, replace the plastic wrap, and let rest for 10 minutes.

FILLING

⅓ cup **unsalted butter,** at room temperature

½ cup **granulated sugar**

2 teaspoons grated **orange zest**

5. TO MAKE THE FILLING: In a medium bowl, mix together the butter, sugar, and orange zest until blended, and set aside.

6. Lightly grease 16 standard muffin cups with butter or cooking spray and set aside. Using a rolling pin, shape the dough into a 16-by-8-inch rectangle, with a long side toward you. Spread the filling over the dough, leaving a ½-inch border at the far edge. Roll lengthwise, beginning with the long edge closest to you. Moisten the border with water and pinch the ends to form secure seams. Cut the roll into 1-inch slices and place each slice, cut side down, into a prepared muffin cup. Cover with plastic wrap and let rise in a warm, draft-free spot until doubled, 30 to 40 minutes.

7. Preheat the oven to 375°F. Bake in the center of the oven until the rolls are golden, 15 to 20 minutes. Cool the rolls in the muffin cups for 3 to 5 minutes before removing. Serve warm or at room temperature.

My friend Vida Lee Mick is the creative inspiration behind this recipe. For more than 20 years, she owned the Uptown Broiler, a popular café in Portland, Oregon. The day before Thanksgiving, a line would form around the block as people waited to pick up a pie (or two or three) so good that they could call it "homemade."

The original recipe is still kept under wraps, but Vida Lee did let it slip that the secret ingredient is a bit of Mapleine. She said—and she is right—that the maple flavoring acts like salt, enhancing the other flavors, and if it is missing, you know it. In this recipe, true maple syrup and a dash of Mapleine blend together to work their magic. To garnish the pie, I fashion a flurry of maple leaves from the leftover pastry and place them on top of the pie after it is cooled. (And, when hurried, I'll use a purchased, unbaked, frozen piecrust.)

MAKES ONE 9-INCH PIE, SERVING 6 TO 8

Vida Lee's Maple Pumpkin Pie

CRUST

1¼ cups **all-purpose flour**

½ teaspoon **salt**

5 tablespoons cold **vegetable shortening,** cut into small pieces

¼ cup cold **unsalted butter,** cut into small pieces

4 to 5 tablespoons **ice water**

continued

1. TO MAKE THE CRUST. In a medium bowl, whisk together the flour and salt. Add the shortening and butter. Using your fingers or a pastry blender, work the shortening and butter into the flour mixture until crumbly and some pea-size pieces of fat remain. If time permits, chill the flour mixture for 30 minutes.

2. Drizzle the ice water over the flour mixture, 1 tablespoon at a time, mixing until all the flour is moistened and the pastry just clears the side of the bowl (adding an additional 1 to 2 teaspoons water if needed). Using lightly floured hands, gather the dough into a ball. Shape into a disk, wrap in plastic wrap, and chill for 1 hour.

continued

FILLING

1 can (15 ounces) **plain pumpkin purée**

½ cup **granulated sugar**

¼ cup firmly packed **light brown sugar**

1 teaspoon **ground cinnamon**

1 teaspoon **ground ginger**

¼ teaspoon **ground cloves**

½ teaspoon **salt**

1¼ cups **half-and-half**

¼ cup **real maple syrup**

2 **eggs**, lightly beaten

¼ teaspoon or more **Mapleine** or other **maple extract**

TOPPING

1 cup chilled **heavy (whipping) cream**

¼ cup **real maple syrup**

3. Remove the dough from the refrigerator and, if needed, soften slightly for easier handling. Roll the dough out to a 12-inch circle on a lightly floured board, between 2 sheets of parchment paper or heavy-duty plastic wrap, or on a pastry cloth with a cloth-covered rolling pin. Transfer the dough to a 9-inch deep-dish pie pan, easing it into the pan. Trim the overhanging edge of the pastry along the pan's edge. Chill for 30 minutes.

4. To make the pastry leaves, roll the extra piecrust dough ⅛ inch thick. Using a maple leaf cookie cutter, cut out 6 to 7 leaves. Using a knife, incise the lines of the leaf. Transfer the leaves to a small baking sheet. To give the appearance and shape of falling leaves, use small wads of foil under each leaf as support, then turn up the ends or sides of the leaf. Chill until baking time.

5. TO MAKE THE FILLING: Preheat the oven to 350°F.

6. In the bowl of a food processor, pulse the pumpkin purée, granulated and brown sugars, cinnamon, ginger, cloves, and salt. Transfer to a 3-quart saucepan. Over medium heat, cook the pumpkin mixture, stirring constantly, until thick and hot, about 5 minutes. Whisk in the half-and-half and maple syrup. Remove from the heat and whisk in the eggs until blended, adding the maple flavoring to taste.

7. Place the prepared pie shell on a baking sheet. Pour the filling into the chilled pie shell. Bake in the lower third of the oven until the filling is puffed and a knife inserted near the center comes out clean, about 60 minutes. Bake the leaves on an upper shelf until the tips just start to turn golden, about 15 minutes. Transfer the leaves and the pie to a rack to cool for at least 1 hour.

8. TO MAKE THE TOPPING: In a chilled bowl, beat the cream until stiff. As the cream begins to thicken, gradually drizzle in the maple syrup. Continue beating until the cream is softly to moderately whipped.

9. To serve, garnish the cooled pie with the maple leaves and serve with the topping. The pie is best eaten within a few hours. Immediately refrigerate any remaining pie, and eat within 1 day.

This rustic, full-flavored tart, with its showcase of dried fruit and autumn spices, is an ideal accompaniment to the traditional Thanksgiving pumpkin pie. After dinner, serve a wedge with rich CARDAMOM CUSTARD SAUCE (recipe follows) or ROSEMARY WHITE CHOCOLATE GANACHE (page 56). In the morning, you'll find that a slice with a double americano is better than breakfast.

MAKES ONE 9-INCH TART, SERVING 8

Rustic Dried Fruit Tart

FILLING

¾ cup (about 4 ounces) coarsely chopped mixed **dried fruit,** loosely packed (see Note)

½ cup **dried cranberries**

2 tablespoons **golden raisins**

2 thick slices **bacon** (2 ounces uncooked), coarsely chopped

2 tablespoons firmly packed **dark** or **light brown sugar**

1 teaspoon grated **lemon zest**

1 teaspoon grated **orange zest**

½ teaspoon **ground nutmeg**

½ teaspoon **ground allspice**

2 to 3 tablespoons **brandy**

½ cup fresh **orange juice**

continued

1. TO MAKE THE FILLING: In a 1-quart saucepan, combine the mixed dried fruit, cranberries, golden raisins, bacon, brown sugar, lemon zest, orange zest, nutmeg, allspice, brandy, and orange juice. Bring to a simmer over medium heat. Simmer, stirring frequently, until the liquid is reduced and thickened but the mixture is still moist and juicy, 3 to 4 minutes. Let cool.

2. TO MAKE THE CRUST: In a medium bowl, whisk together the flour and salt. (If time permits, chill the bowl and flour mixture for 30 minutes before using.) Using the large holes of a grater, grate the butter and shortening into the flour mixture. (The frozen fat is easier to incorporate into the dry ingredients and remains cold for a flakier crust.) Using your fingers or a pastry blender, work the butter and shortening into the flour mixture until crumbly. Sprinkle in the ice water, beginning with 3 tablespoons, and mix until the dough holds together when pressed. Shape into a disk, wrap in plastic wrap, and chill for 1 hour.

3. Preheat the oven to 375°F. Line a baking sheet with parchment paper.

4. Place the dough on a lightly floured surface and roll it into a 12-inch circle. (It doesn't have to be perfect.) Spread the filling on the dough, leaving a 1½-inch border. With moistened fingers, fold the uncovered dough up and over the filling to create pleats. Lightly press the pleats together. Dip a pastry brush into water, moisten the edges of the crust, and sprinkle with the granulated sugar.

continued

Rustic Dried Fruit Tart *continued*

CRUST

1¼ cups **all-purpose flour**

½ teaspoon **salt**

6 tablespoons frozen **unsalted butter**

2 tablespoons frozen **vegetable shortening**

4 tablespoons or more **ice water**

1 tablespoon **granulated sugar**

CARDAMOM CUSTARD SAUCE (facing page) or **ROSEMARY WHITE CHOCOLATE GANACHE** (page 56) for serving

5. Bake until the crust is golden, about 30 minutes. (If the fruit begins to brown, cover it with aluminum foil.) Slip the parchment paper and tart onto a wire rack to cool. Serve warm or at room temperature with custard sauce or ganache.

NOTE: The quality of the dried fruit makes a difference here. If possible, look for unsulfured dried fruit. If you can't find it and time is of the essence, use the prepackaged mixed dried fruit available in supermarkets. A premium brand typically comes in an 8-ounce package containing pitted prunes, dried apples, apricots, peaches, and pears.

CARDAMOM CUSTARD SAUCE

This spicy–sweet custard sauce has the seductive aroma
and flavor of whole cardamom seeds, a spice native to India and
a member of the ginger family. **MAKES 2 CUPS**

3 whole **cardamom pods,** crushed

2 cups **half-and-half**

4 **egg yolks,** at room temperature

3 tablespoons **granulated sugar**

$\frac{1}{4}$ teaspoon pure **vanilla extract**

In a heavy, medium saucepan, over medium-high heat, bring the cardamom pods
and half-and-half to a boil. Meanwhile, in a medium bowl, whisk together the egg
yolks and sugar until smooth, pale yellow, and thick, about 1 minute. Slowly whisk
the boiling cream into the egg mixture until blended, then pour the mixture back
into the saucepan and cook over medium-high heat, whisking constantly, until the
sauce thickens and covers the back of a spoon, 6 to 10 minutes. Strain through a
fine-mesh sieve into a clean container. Stir in the vanilla. Serve warm or chilled.

Like no other quick bread or cake, gingerbread goes hand in hand with holidays. It's always a welcome contribution to the menu, so consider it the next time you're invited to Thanksgiving dinner and want to take along a treat.

The synergy of warm spices and dark molasses gives this rich gingerbread a come-back-for-more reputation. It's an heirloom recipe, with each baker adding a personal touch: a dash of cocoa to bring out a deep and subtle flavor, ginger to add a peppery zing, or blackstrap molasses, the boldest molasses of all.

To serve, top the gingerbread with an English-style sticky caramel topping (see the variation), or finish with sweetened whipped cream, a few spoonfuls of lemon curd, or pan-seared and sugar-dipped slices of tart apple.

MAKES ONE 8-INCH-SQUARE CAKE, SERVING 9 TO 12

The Ultimate Dinner Guest's Gingerbread

1½ cups **all-purpose** flour

1 teaspoon **baking soda**

½ teaspoon **salt**

1 teaspoon **ground cinnamon**

¼ teaspoon **ground cloves**

2 teaspoons **unsweetened Dutch process cocoa powder**

2 **eggs,** at room temperature

1. Preheat the oven to 350°F. Grease an 8-by-8-inch baking dish lightly with cooking spray and set aside.

2. Into a medium bowl, sift together the flour, baking soda, salt, cinnamon, cloves, and cocoa, then lightly whisk and set aside. (If substituting ground ginger for the freshly grated ginger called for later in the recipe, sift it in now with the other spices.)

3. In a stand mixer set on medium speed, beat the eggs until foamy. Beat in the brown sugar until light and lump free. Beat in the buttermilk, molasses, butter, and fresh ginger until well blended, scraping down the sides and bottom of the bowl as necessary. Turn off the mixer, add the flour mixture, and on low speed, beat until just blended. Pour the batter into the prepared pan. Smack the pan down on the counter once or twice to release any air bubbles. Next, gently rotate the pan to settle and level the batter. Bake until the top springs back when lightly touched and the edges have pulled away from the sides, 30 to 40 minutes. Transfer to a rack to cool for 10 minutes. Serve warm or at room temperature.

½ cup firmly packed **dark brown sugar**

½ cup **buttermilk**

½ cup **dark** or **blackstrap molasses**

½ cup **unsalted butter,** melted and cooled

1 tablespoon **grated fresh ginger,** or 2½ teaspoons **ground ginger**

• • •

VARIATIONS

1. For Sticky-Top Gingerbread, follow the main recipe, letting the cake cool while preparing the topping. Place an oven rack 4 to 5 inches from the broiler's heat source. Preheat the broiler.

2. To make the topping, in a small saucepan over medium heat, combine 3 tablespoons **unsalted butter,** ⅓ cup firmly packed **dark brown sugar,** and 2 tablespoons **heavy (whipping) cream,** stirring constantly as the mixture bubbles and then thickens, about 5 minutes. Remove from the heat and pour over the warm gingerbread, letting the topping seep down the sides.

3. Place the gingerbread under the broiler and broil until the topping is bubbling, about 40 seconds. Watch carefully to prevent the topping from burning. Serve warm with lightly sweetened whipped cream.

For gingerbread lovers who crave those semisweet morsels, be sure to try Chocolate Chip Gingerbread Cupcakes. Follow the main recipe, lining a standard muffin tin with paper or foil liners. Increase the cocoa from 2 teaspoons to 1 tablespoon and use the 2½ teaspoons ground ginger instead of the fresh ginger. Proceed as directed. After the batter is blended, stir in 1 cup **semisweet chocolate chips.** Divide the batter evenly among the muffin cups. Bake in the center of the oven until the tops spring back when lightly pressed with a fingertip, about 20 minutes. Do not overbake. Cool the cupcakes in the tin for 5 minutes, then transfer to a rack to cool. Serve plain or dusted with **powdered sugar,** warm or at room temperature.

At my grandmother's house, the long Thanksgiving weekend featured leftover turkey in its many disguises, followed by a different dessert every night. My favorite was the apple crisp, its hot fruit bubbling under a brown sugar and oat topping. The crisp turned out differently each time, depending on who picked the apples from the grove of trees that surrounded Nanny's victory garden. As a young apple picker, I learned that the ideal crisp includes at least four different kinds of apples, each adding its own flavor and texture to the filling. Today, with heirloom apples showing up in produce aisles and farmers' markets, you'll be able to pick and choose from a welcome variety.

SERVES 4 TO 6

FILLING

4 to 6 **medium baking apples of different varieties,** peeled, cored, and thinly sliced

Juice of ½ medium **lemon**

⅓ cup **granulated sugar**

Backyard Apple Tree Crisp

TOPPING

⅔ cup **all-purpose flour**

½ cup **old-fashioned rolled oats**

¾ cup firmly packed **light brown sugar**

¼ cup **granulated sugar**

1 tablespoon **ground cinnamon**

½ cup **unsalted butter,** cut into small pieces

Vanilla ice cream, warm CARDAMOM CUSTARD SAUCE (page 39), or ROSEMARY WHITE CHOCOLATE GANACHE (page 56) for serving

1. Preheat the oven to 350°F. Generously butter an 8-by-8-inch baking dish or another 2-quart baking dish and set aside.

2. TO MAKE THE FILLING: In a medium bowl, toss together the apples, lemon juice, and sugar. Transfer the apples to the baking dish and set aside.

3. TO MAKE THE TOPPING: In a medium bowl, mix together the flour, oats, brown sugar, granulated sugar, and cinnamon. Using your fingers or a pastry blender, work the butter into the flour mixture until it resembles coarse crumbs.

4. Sprinkle the topping over the apples. Bake in the center of the oven until the crisp is golden brown and the apples are bubbling around the edges, 35 to 45 minutes. Remove and cool in the pan for 15 minutes. Serve with vanilla ice cream, warm CARDAMOM CUSTARD SAUCE, or ROSEMARY WHITE CHOCOLATE GANACHE.

Hanukkah—the eight-day Festival of Lights—always begins at sunset. Jewish families light the menorah's middle candle, called the Shamash candle, and use it each night to light one of the other eight candles. Then they offer prayers and enjoy traditional food, songs, and games. The celebration commemorates the Jewish Maccabees' victory over the Assyrian army in 165 B.C.E. It also honors the miracle that occurred after the

K I S L E V						
1	2	3	4	5	6	7
8	9	10	11	12	13	14
15	16	17	18	19	20	21
22	23	24	☾	26	27	28
29	30	31				

Jews regained their temple, which the Assyrians had taken over to use as a temple to Zeus. The temple priests found enough purified olive oil to keep the temple's menorah burning for only one day, but miraculously the oil lasted for eight days. Hanukkah (also written Hannuka, Hanukah, or Chanukah), which usually falls in December, has less religious significance than other Jewish holy days, but it is a welcome and well-loved midwinter holiday.

HANUKKAH

CYCLICAL, BASED ON THE LUNAR CALENDAR:
THE 25TH DAY OF THE
JEWISH MONTH OF KISLEV

● ● ● ● ● ● ●

Hanukkah Frosted Cookie Cutouts 46
Razzle-Dazzle Dreidels 47

Chocolate Gelt Hide-a-Cookies 48
Chocolate Almond Cinnamon Stars 51

Apricot Nut or Cardamom Pistachio Rugelach 52
Rugelach with Marmalade, Sage, and Pine Nuts 53

Pear-Apple Strudel with
Rosemary White Chocolate Ganache 54

Jerusalem Olive Oil Cake with
Orange Marmalade and Almonds 57

Streusel-Top Sour Cream Coffee Cake 60

Bubbee and Me Baked Candy Apples 62

Selma's Apricot Noodle Kugel 64

Golden Savory Cheese Coins 65

A Nice Little Cheesecake 66

"Let's Make a Dreidel" Chocolate Cake 68

Erna Neuman's family insists on frosted sugar cookie cutouts for the Hanukkah celebration, and Erna's are some of the best. In her Southern California home, whoever stops by the week or so before festivities begin gets to help cut out stars, dreidels, and other Hanukkah-shaped cookies, decorate them with blue and white frostings, then enjoy finished cookies turned out in Hanukkah colors.

If you have a can of powdered buttermilk in your pantry to substitute for the fresh buttermilk, everything you'll need to make this recipe is cupboard close and refrigerator ready. You can easily make the dough in advance, so that when the time is right, the kids in your life can roll, cut, frost, and munch to their hearts' content.

MAKES ABOUT 3 DOZEN 3-INCH COOKIES

Hanukkah Frosted Cookie Cutouts

DOUGH

2 ¼ cups **all-purpose flour**

½ teaspoon **baking soda**

¼ teaspoon **salt**

½ cup **unsalted butter,** at room temperature

⅔ cup **baker's** or **superfine sugar,** plus more for sprinkling (see Note)

1 **egg,** at room temperature, lightly beaten

2 teaspoons **pure vanilla extract**

¼ cup **buttermilk,** at room temperature

1. TO MAKE THE DOUGH: Into a medium bowl, sift together the flour, baking soda, and salt, then lightly whisk and set aside.

2. In a stand mixer set on low speed, beat the butter until creamy, about 30 seconds. On medium speed, beat in the sugar until light and fluffy. Add the egg and beat until well blended, scraping down the sides and bottom of the bowl as necessary. Beat in the vanilla until blended. Add half of the flour mixture, then the buttermilk, then the remaining flour, beating until it is combined and forms a dough.

3. Using lightly floured hands, gather the sticky dough into a ball. Divide the ball in half and flatten each into a 6- to 8-inch disk. Wrap each disk in plastic wrap and chill for 2 hours or until firm.

4. Preheat the oven to 375°F. Line a baking sheet with parchment paper or leave ungreased, and set aside.

ERNA NEUMAN'S ICING

3 cups **powdered sugar**

⅓ cup **unsalted butter,**
at room temperature

Pinch of **salt**

1 teaspoon **pure vanilla extract**

½ teaspoon **pure lemon extract**

2 tablespoons **whole milk** or
cream, plus more if needed

2 to 3 drops **blue food coloring**

5. Remove the dough from the refrigerator and, if needed, soften slightly for easier handling. Roll the dough out ⅛ inch thick on a lightly floured board, between 2 sheets of parchment paper or heavy-duty plastic wrap, or on a pastry cloth with a cloth-covered rolling pin.

6. Lightly dip a 3- or 3½-inch Hanukkah-themed cookie cutter in flour, then firmly press it straight down into the dough. Repeat, cutting the cookies close together to avoid rerolling. Using a spatula, carefully transfer the cookies to the baking sheet, spacing them 1 inch apart.

7. Bake until golden, about 14 minutes. Cool slightly on the baking sheet before transferring to a wire rack to cool completely.

8. TO MAKE THE ICING: In a medium bowl, beat together the powdered sugar, butter, salt, vanilla, and lemon extract until blended. It will be lumpy. Stir in the milk until it reaches a spreading consistency. If desired, divide the icing in half and add blue food coloring to one half, mixing until the color is uniform. Using a small spatula, spread the blue icing over the cooled cookies. Place the white icing in a pastry bag fitted with a star tip and pipe designs, or spread the white icing over the cooled cookies and decorate as desired.

NOTE: Baker's or superfine sugar is available in supermarket baking sections. For a quick substitute, whirl 1 cup of granulated sugar at a time in a food processor or blender until fine, about 20 seconds.

• • •

VARIATION
Add glitter to your Hanukkah table with Razzle-Dazzle Dreidels. Follow the main recipe, using a dreidel cookie cutter. Before baking, use a clean watercolor brush to paint the cookies with an egg-white wash (1 **egg white** lightly beaten with 2 teaspoons **water**). Cover the painted areas with blue-colored sugar. Continue as directed.

You don't have to wait until Hanukkah to make these chocolate coin-shaped shortbread cookies, but they're a scrumptious way to satisfy your holiday sweet tooth before you take a spin on the dreidel. For a festive way to stash the cookies if you want to use them as a party favor or hostess gift, let the kids help you make a decorative paper container that resembles a Shamash, the candle used to light the other candles in the menorah.

To make each coin the same size and shape, try the clever toilet-paper tube technique. You'll be surprised how easy and convenient it is. (And the handy throwaway cardboard tubes also are ideal for molding the dough before storing it in the freezer.)

MAKES ABOUT 6 DOZEN COOKIES

Chocolate Gelt Hide-a-Cookies

1 empty **toilet-paper roll**

2 cups **cake flour**

½ cup **unsweetened Dutch process cocoa powder**

¼ teaspoon **salt**

1 cup **unsalted butter,** at room temperature

1 cup **baker's** or **superfine sugar** (see page 12)

1 teaspoon **pure vanilla extract**

Shamash cookie container (optional; see page 50)

1. TO MAKE THE COOKIE MOLD, make a straight cut down the length of the toilet-paper tube. Draw a line 1¼ inches from one of the long edges and overlap the edges to that line to make a smaller diameter tube. Tape closed.

2. Into a medium bowl, sift together the flour, cocoa, and salt, then lightly whisk and set aside.

3. In a stand mixer or with a hand mixer set on low speed, beat the butter until creamy, about 30 seconds. On medium speed, add the sugar and beat until light and fluffy. Beat in the vanilla until well blended, scraping down the sides and bottom of the bowl as necessary. Turn off the mixer, add half the flour mixture, and beat on low speed until blended. Add the remaining flour and beat until blended. Gather the sticky dough into a ball and divide into 5 equal portions.

continued

4. Roll each portion into a cylinder, approximately 4½ inches long and 1½ inches in diameter. Center each cylinder of dough on a piece of plastic wrap and roll to seal. Pack the dough tightly into the mold tube. Pull the end of the plastic wrap to remove the dough from the tube. Twist the plastic wrap to seal the ends. Place in the freezer for 30 to 60 minutes.

5. Preheat the oven to 300°F. Line a baking sheet with parchment paper or grease it lightly and set aside.

6. Using a ruler, mark ⅜-inch increments on the dough cylinders. Slice the dough and place the cookies on the prepared baking sheet. Using the tines of a fork, prick the center of each cookie clear through to the bottom. Bake until firm to the touch, about 20 minutes. Cool slightly on the baking sheet before transferring to a wire rack to cool completely. Store in an airtight container.

NOTE: Baker's or superfine sugar is available in supermarket baking sections. For a quick substitute, whirl 1 cup of granulated sugar at a time in a food processor or blender until fine, about 20 seconds.

TO CREATE A SHAMASH COOKIE CONTAINER, glue two 5-by-12-inch strips of bright blue construction paper together short end to short end. Roll the glued strips into a tube approximately 2 inches across. Glue in place. Center one 3-inch white construction paper circle over one tube end. Fold the circle's paper edge over the tube's edge and glue in place. Meanwhile, stack 10 cookies, then wrap the stack in plastic wrap and seal. Stand the tube up on its papered end and slip the cookie parcel inside. This recipe will fill 6 to 8 containers.

TO CREATE THE CANDLE'S WICK AND FLAME, pierce a tiny hole in the center of a second white construction paper circle. Twist a small knot at the end of a 3-inch length of pipe cleaner and thread the unknotted end from the inside to the outside of the hole. Finish the unknotted end with a construction or tissue paper "flame," and glue in place. Center the paper circle and its wick over the open end of the filled tube. Fold the circle's paper edge over the tube's edge and glue in place.

• • •

VARIATION

1. Bake a batch of Chocolate Almond Cinnamon Stars to twinkle along-side other holiday cookies at your next Hanukkah gathering. Follow the main recipe, decreasing the vanilla to ½ teaspoon and adding ½ teaspoon **almond extract.** After gathering the dough into a ball, divide the ball in half and flatten each half into a 6- to 8-inch disk. Roll out the first disk ⅛ inch thick on a lightly floured board, between 2 sheets of parchment paper or heavy-duty plastic wrap, or on a pastry cloth with a cloth-covered rolling pin. Preheat the oven to 350°F.

2. Use a 2½-inch star cookie cutter. Before baking, generously sprinkle the cookies with **plain** or **cinnamon sugar** (1 teaspoon **cinnamon** mixed with ¼ cup **baker's sugar**), and bake for 10 to 12 minutes. Makes about 4½ dozen cookies.

Just saying "rugelach" brings a smile to the face of most cookie lovers. This recipe, with its choice of either a sweet apricot nut or a festive cardamom pistachio filling, will have them grinning from ear to ear. Rugelach, made with a rich cream cheese dough, has a special Hanukkah connection.

Early Hebrew writing from the Maccabean period tells a folktale about the Israelite widow Judith, who plied the commander of the Assyrian army with cheesecake and wine. When he dozed off, she cut off his head. His soldiers wasted no time in leaving, and Judith's people were set free. In many Hanukkah foods, the cream cheese symbolizes Judith's fearlessness and victory over her enemies.

Remember, the dough needs to chill overnight, so plan accordingly. Also, don't forget to choose one filling, not both, since each makes enough for 3 dozen cookies.

MAKES ABOUT 3 DOZEN COOKIES

Apricot Nut or Cardamom Pistachio Rugelach

PASTRY

2 cups sifted **all-purpose flour**

½ teaspoon **salt**

1 cup **unsalted butter,** at room temperature

8 ounces **cream cheese,** at room temperature

1. TO MAKE THE PASTRY: The night before baking, in a medium bowl, whisk together the flour and salt until blended.

2. In a stand mixer set on medium speed, beat the butter and cream cheese until smooth and creamy. On low speed, gradually beat in the flour mixture until just combined. Scrape down the sides and bottom of the bowl as necessary. Scrape the mixture onto a lightly floured board, and using floured hands, form a 6-by-3-inch log. Cut the log into thirds (8 ounces each) and press each portion into a round, flat disk. On the countertop, spread two 14-inch lengths of plastic wrap, overlapping them by 4 inches. Place one disk in the center and cover with 2 more sheets in the same manner. Place the rolling pin in the center of the disk, then roll firmly and evenly out to the edge. Continue rolling in this fashion until the dough is a 12-inch circle. Repeat with the remaining disks of dough. Leave the dough in the plastic wrap, seal, stack, and refrigerate overnight.

3. The next day, when you are ready to bake, preheat the oven to 350°F. Line a baking sheet with parchment paper or foil.

APRICOT NUT FILLING

½ cup firmly packed **light brown sugar**

1 tablespoon **ground cinnamon**

1 cup **apricot preserves**

½ cup **walnuts**, finely chopped

½ cup **pecans**, finely chopped

¾ cup **raisins**, chopped

CARDAMOM PISTACHIO FILLING

½ cup firmly packed **light brown sugar**

½ teaspoon **ground cardamom**

3 tablespoons **unsalted butter**, melted

1 cup **pistachios**, finely chopped

¾ cup **golden raisins**, chopped

Milk for brushing

Granulated sugar for sprinkling

4. TO MAKE THE APRICOT NUT FILLING: In a small bowl, mix together the brown sugar and cinnamon until blended. Remove one round of dough from the refrigerator and peel off the top layer of plastic wrap. Lightly flour the top of the dough and flip it over onto a work surface. Brush the top of the dough with one-third of the apricot preserves. Sprinkle one-third of the brown sugar-cinnamon mixture over the preserves, then sprinkle with one-third of the walnuts, one-third of the pecans, and one-third of the raisins. Lightly press any loose nuts into the dough.

TO MAKE THE CARDAMOM PISTACHIO FILLING: In a small bowl, mix together the brown sugar and cardamom until blended. Remove one round of dough from the refrigerator and peel off the top layer of plastic wrap. Brush the top of the dough with one-third of the melted butter. Sprinkle one-third of the brown sugar–cardamom mixture over the butter, then sprinkle with one-third of the pistachios and one-third of the raisins. Lightly press any loose nuts into the dough.

5. Using a long, sharp knife, cut the dough into 12 pie-shaped wedges. Starting with the wide end opposite the point and working quickly, roll each wedge up jelly-roll fashion. Arrange the rolls, with the point side down, 1 inch apart on the baking sheet. Brush the tops and sides of the rugelach with milk and sprinkle with the granulated sugar. Bake until golden brown and lightly puffy, about 30 minutes. Let the cookies firm and cool slightly on the baking sheet before transferring them to a rack to cool completely. Repeat with the remaining 2 rounds of dough.

• • •

VARIATION

To make Rugelach with Marmalade, Sage, and Pine Nuts, follow the recipe for the pastry, mixing 1 tablespoon finely chopped **fresh sage leaves** and 1 teaspoon grated **orange zest** into the blended butter and cream cheese mixture before adding the flour mixture. Follow the recipe for the apricot nut filling, omitting the brown sugar and cinnamon. Substitute 1 cup warm **marmalade** for the apricot preserves and use 1 cup **pine nuts** instead of the pecans and walnuts. Proceed as directed.

Nothing is quite as good as homemade strudel, and today anyone can make it. In my grandmother's time, making strudel was a major event. The dining room table became kitchen central, and a long bedsheet became a temporary pastry cloth so the homemade strudel dough could be stretched tissue-thin. My mother had the convenience of ready-made pastry sheets from the neighborhood deli or bakery. Now, thank goodness, we can find frozen phyllo pastry at the supermarket. It makes a quick and deliciously flaky envelope for the wonderful pear-apple filling.

The strudel is served with an elegantly assertive ganache made with white chocolate, fresh rosemary, and cream. This unforgettably rich and mysterious sauce will dress up any homemade fruit dessert. Try it on the BACKYARD APPLE TREE CRISP (page 43) or the RUSTIC DRIED FRUIT TART (page 37), and you'll see what I mean.

MAKES ABOUT TWELVE 1½-INCH SLICES

Pear-Apple Strudel
with Rosemary White Chocolate Ganache

FILLING

2 medium to large **Granny Smith apples,** peeled, cored, and cut into ½-inch cubes

2 medium to large **Comice pears,** peeled, cored, and cut into ½-inch cubes

1 tablespoon **water**

2 tablespoons **granulated sugar**

½ teaspoon **ground cinnamon**

1. TO MAKE THE FILLING: In a large skillet over medium heat, combine the apples, pears, and water. Sprinkle the sugar and cinnamon over the apples. Cook the fruit mixture, tossing often, until the apples are partially cooked, about 5 minutes. As the mixture releases its juices, remove 2 tablespoons of the juice and set aside to cool. (If there is not enough juice, you can use water instead.)

2. Mix the cornstarch and the reserved juice (or 2 tablespoons of water). Add to the filling and stir over medium-high heat until the filling thickens, about 1 minute. Remove from the heat and stir in the dates, if desired, the lemon and orange zests, and the liqueur, and set aside.

FILLING *continued*

1 tablespoon **cornstarch**

1 cup chopped **dates** (optional)

1 teaspoon grated **lemon zest**

1 teaspoon grated **orange zest**

2 to 3 tablespoons **Grand Marnier** or other **orange-flavored liqueur**

STRUDEL

½ cup toasted **hazelnuts**, finely chopped

½ cup coarse **graham cracker crumbs**

2 tablespoons **granulated sugar**

Six 17-by-12-inch sheets **phyllo pastry**, fresh or frozen (thawed if frozen)

6 tablespoons **unsalted butter**, melted

ROSEMARY WHITE CHOCOLATE GANACHE (page 56) for serving

3. TO MAKE THE STRUDEL: Preheat the oven to 375°F. Line a baking sheet with parchment paper or butter it lightly and set aside. In a bowl, mix together the hazelnuts, graham cracker crumbs, and sugar.

4. Place a dry kitchen towel on a work surface, with the long side toward you. On the towel, place 1 phyllo sheet with its long edge right up against the far long edge of the towel (this makes it easier to slide the full strudel onto the baking sheet). Place the remaining sheets under a damp towel. Brush the phyllo lightly with melted butter. Top with a second phyllo sheet, then brush with butter. Sprinkle with about 3 tablespoons of the hazelnut mixture. Continue with 3 more phyllo sheets, brushing each with butter and sprinkling each with about 3 tablespoons of the hazelnut mixture. Top with the remaining phyllo sheet and brush with butter.

5. Using a slotted spoon, place the filling on top of the phyllo in a 3-inch strip about 2½ inches from the bottom edge, leaving about 2 inches from each short side uncovered. Fold the short edges over the filling. Fold the long end closest to you over the filling and continue to roll, using the towel as a guide. Gently nudge the strudel, seam side down, onto the prepared baking sheet. Brush the strudel with butter, and cut three or four 1-inch vents into the top.

6. Bake the strudel until golden, about 45 minutes. Let cool for 10 minutes, then, using a serrated knife, cut into 1½-inch slices. To serve, drizzle the ganache over each slice, and be sure to have more ganache ready to pass.

ROSEMARY WHITE CHOCOLATE GANACHE

When you combine heavy cream and white chocolate with
fresh rosemary, you create an incredible flavor that makes a rich,
delicious, and elegant dessert sauce. MAKES ABOUT 2 CUPS

¾ cup **heavy (whipping) cream**

½ cup packed **fresh rosemary**

8 ounces **white chocolate,**
broken into small pieces

2 tablespoons **unsalted butter**

Pinch of **salt**

In a medium saucepan over medium heat, bring the cream and rosemary to a boil.
Remove from the heat, cover, and let infuse for 10 to 15 minutes. Meanwhile,
place the chocolate in a medium bowl. Bring the cream to a second boil. Strain
out the rosemary, then pour the hot cream over the chocolate. Let stand for 3 to
4 minutes, then whisk until smooth. It will be like a thin sauce. Stir in the butter
and salt. If making the ganache ahead, cover with plastic wrap and chill.

The Hanukkah story tells us that when the Jewish priests prepared to rededicate their temple, they could find only a day's worth of purified olive oil to rekindle the menorah's "eternal flame." Even so, the flame burned for eight days and nights. Symbolic of the miracle at the heart of the Hanukkah tradition, olive oil has become an important ingredient in foods related to the holiday.

Typically, the oil is used to fry food during Hanukkah. In this recipe, however, we use it as an ingredient in a delicious citrus-scented holiday cake, which can be served as a coffee cake at breakfast or as a simple dessert after supper. (By the way, this baked delight is thoroughly ecumenical. In Spain, early convent kitchens made a similar cake at Christmas. It was split horizontally and filled with whipped cream sweetened with sugar and a dash of brandy.)

The olive oil in this cake makes it extra moist, and its flavor enlivens and accentuates the other ingredients. Be sure to use a fruity olive oil (put a drop on your finger and give it a taste test).

MAKES ONE 9-INCH CAKE, SERVING 9

Jerusalem Olive Oil Cake
with Orange Marmalade and Almonds

1¼ cups **all-purpose flour**

¼ teaspoon **baking powder**

¼ teaspoon **baking soda**

continued

1. Preheat the oven to 350°F. Lightly grease the bottom and sides of a 9-inch round cake pan with cooking spray. Line the bottom with a round of parchment or waxed paper. Grease the paper lightly and set aside.

2. In a medium bowl, whisk together the flour, baking powder, baking soda, and salt. Set aside.

continued

Jerusalem Olive Oil Cake *continued*

¼ teaspoon **salt**

2 **eggs,** at room temperature

1 cup **granulated sugar**

½ cup fruity **extra-virgin olive oil**

¾ cup **milk**

1½ tablespoons grated **orange zest** (from about 3 medium oranges)

¼ to ⅓ cup sliced **almonds**

2 tablespoons **marmalade,** warmed in the microwave

1 tablespoon **powdered sugar**

3. In a medium bowl, whisk together the eggs and sugar until well blended, about 1 minute. Whisk in the olive oil, milk, and orange zest. Whisk the egg mixture into the flour mixture until thoroughly blended. Pour the batter into the prepared pan and bake until the cake is firm and a toothpick inserted into the center comes out clean, about 30 minutes. Transfer the pan to a rack to cool for 20 minutes.

4. Meanwhile, scatter the almonds in a single layer on a small baking sheet or pan and toast in the oven until slightly brown, 8 to 10 minutes.

5. To serve, unmold the cake, remove the parchment paper, and place the cake on a flat serving plate. Using a pastry brush, coat the sides of the cake and a 1-inch rim along the top with the warm marmalade, arranging any bits of peel along the rim. (If the marmalade is too thick, add ¼ teaspoon warm water and stir.) Press the almonds onto the sticky top rim. Using a fine sieve, lightly dust the powdered sugar evenly over the top. Serve warm or at room temperature.

This is one of the simplest and best coffee cakes my mother used to bake for the family on Sunday mornings. She always made the sweet streusel crumb topping extra thick because she knew how much I loved it.

MAKES ONE 8-INCH CAKE, SERVING 8

Streusel-Top Sour Cream Coffee Cake

TOPPING

1 tablespoon **all-purpose flour**

⅓ cup firmly packed **light brown sugar**

1 teaspoon **ground cinnamon**

2 tablespoons cold **unsalted butter,** cut into pea-size pieces

¾ cup **chopped walnuts** and **pecans**

CAKE

1⅓ cups **all-purpose flour**

¾ teaspoon **baking powder**

½ teaspoon **baking soda**

½ teaspoon **salt**

6 tablespoons unsalted **butter,** at room temperature

⅓ cup **granulated sugar**

¼ cup firmly packed **light brown sugar**

1 **egg**

¾ teaspoon **pure vanilla extract**

¾ cup **sour cream**

1. Preheat the oven to 350°F. Grease an 8-by-8-inch baking pan lightly and set aside.

2. TO MAKE THE TOPPING: In a medium bowl, whisk together the flour, brown sugar, and cinnamon until blended. Using your fingers or a pastry blender, work the butter into the flour mixture until the topping is crumbly. Stir in the walnuts and pecans and set aside.

3. TO MAKE THE CAKE BATTER: In a medium bowl, whisk together the flour, baking powder, baking soda, and salt until well blended.

4. In another medium bowl, using a hand mixer set on medium speed, beat the butter until creamy, about 30 seconds. Beat in the granulated and brown sugars until smooth and lump free. Beat in the egg until well blended, scraping down the sides and bottom of the bowl as necessary. Beat in the vanilla until blended. Add the flour mixture in three parts, alternating with the sour cream, beating until just blended. Scrape down the sides and bottom of the bowl. The thick batter should be smooth and blended.

5. Spread the batter into the prepared baking pan and sprinkle the reserved topping over the batter. Bake in the middle of the oven until the cake begins to pull away from the sides and a toothpick inserted in the center comes out clean, about 35 minutes. Let the cake cool in the pan for at least 10 minutes. Cut into squares and serve. The coffee cake is best served slightly warm, but it keeps well, wrapped, for 1 or 2 days at room temperature.

Your grandmas and grandpas will remember these candy apples from when they were young. They've been around for a long time. That's because they are easy to make, tasty to eat, and pretty too, and little kids love to help create them. Thanks to Wendy Smolen, deputy editor of *Nick, Jr.* magazine, and her mom, Ethel Weisberg, the recipe's been dusted off and printed here just for you. Your grandkids can help you measure the "red hots" and smoosh them into the apples.

Did you know that in Greece, it is customary to serve apples during Hanukkah? The tradition stems from the belief that the Maccabees feasted on apples and duck to celebrate their victory over the Assyrian king Antiochus IV and his army.

SERVES 6

Bubbee and Me Baked Candy Apples

6 medium **baking apples,** such as Golden Delicious, Rome, or Gravenstein

2 tablespoons **unsalted butter,** divided into 6 pieces

About ⅔ cup **cinnamon imperials,** also known as "red hots"

¾ cup **fresh orange juice**

1. Preheat the oven to 350°F. Using a vegetable peeler, remove a wide strip of peel from the top of each apple. Using an apple corer, scoop out and discard all traces of the core, being careful not to make the cavity too large or to pierce the bottom of the apples.

2. Arrange the apples in a glass baking dish large enough to easily hold them. Using clean fingers, smoosh a piece of butter down into the cavity of each apple. Then divide the ⅔ cup imperials among the cavities, reserving 2 to 3 tablespoons. Pour the orange juice into the bottom of the baking dish and sprinkle the reserved imperials over the juice.

3. Bake, uncovered, basting occasionally with the juice until the apples are tender when pierced with a knife, about 40 minutes. (If desired, during the last 5 minutes of baking, garnish the apples with the reserved "red hots.") Remove from the oven and drizzle some of the baking juices over each apple. Serve with a little of the sauce poured around each apple.

Selma Paul lives in Tucson, Arizona. An attorney for six decades, she is also the matriarch of her kitchen. Except for Passover, no celebration or holiday dinner is complete without her sweet apricot noodle kugel. Now her grown children and their families are scattered throughout the West, and Selma's kugel is gaining fans. Her grandchildren, especially, think it's like having dessert as part of the dinner.

SERVES 8

Selma's Apricot Noodle Kugel

8 ounces **wide egg noodles**

¼ cup **unsalted butter,** at room temperature

3 ounces **cream cheese,** at room temperature

1 cup **sour cream**

3 **eggs,** lightly beaten

1 teaspoon **pure vanilla extract**

¼ teaspoon **salt**

1 cup **apricot preserves,** divided

⅓ cup firmly packed **light brown sugar**

½ cup **pecan halves**

1. Preheat the oven to 350°F. Grease lightly or butter a 9-by-9-inch baking pan and set aside.

2. In a large saucepan, bring lightly salted water to a boil. Stir in the noodles and cook until al dente, 8 to 10 minutes. Drain and rinse under cold water.

3. In a medium bowl, combine the noodles, butter, cream cheese, sour cream, eggs, vanilla, and salt and toss until blended. Spread half the mixture into the prepared baking pan. Dot and spread by spoonfuls ½ cup of the apricot preserves over the noodles. Don't worry about any gaps in the preserves. Spread the remaining noodle mixture over the apricot layer, then dot and spread by spoonfuls the remaining ½ cup apricot preserves. Sprinkle the brown sugar over the surface and arrange the pecan halves on top. Bake until golden and slightly crisp on top, about 40 minutes.

Years ago, I tasted a crisp, cheesy cracker at a Pennsylvania inn. It was served with wine as a simple hors d'oeuvre. In my version, the crackers are shaped like coins, and the unbaked dough is brushed with a turmeric-tinged egg wash to give each cracker a glittery sheen. At Hanukkah, they commemorate the coins minted by the newly independent Maccabee state that was formed after the Assyrians were driven out of Jerusalem.

MAKES ABOUT 6 DOZEN 1½-INCH COINS

Golden Savory Cheese Coins

Pinch of **ground turmeric**

1 tablespoon hot **water**

1½ cups sifted **all-purpose flour**

½ teaspoon **salt**

1 cup grated **Gruyère** or **aged hard goat cheese**

½ cup frozen **unsalted butter**

3 tablespoons **milk**

1 **egg yolk**

1. Preheat the oven to 350°F. Line a baking sheet with parchment paper or leave ungreased, and set aside. In a small bowl, sprinkle the turmeric over the hot water and set aside.

2. In a medium bowl, whisk together the flour, salt, and cheese. Using the large holes of a grater, grate the butter into the flour mixture (the frozen fat is easier to incorporate into the dry ingredients and remains cold for a flakier coin). Using your fingers or a pastry blender, work the butter into the flour mixture until crumbly.

3. Drizzle the milk over the flour mixture, stirring until it forms large lumps. Transfer the mixture from the bowl into a plastic bag. Quickly push the dough together until it forms a flaky ball. Flatten into a 9-inch disk and chill, in the bag, for at least 1 hour.

4. Roll the dough out ¼ inch thick on a lightly floured board, between 2 sheets of parchment paper or heavy-duty plastic wrap, or on a pastry cloth with a cloth-covered rolling pin.

5. Lightly dip a 1½-inch round garnish or mini-biscuit cutter in flour, then firmly press it straight down into the dough. Repeat, cutting the coins close together to avoid rerolling. Using a spatula, carefully transfer the coins to the baking sheet.

6. Beat the egg yolk into the reserved turmeric mixture, then brush the mixture over the surface of each coin. Bake until the coins are lightly browned and have a golden shine, about 25 minutes. Transfer to a rack to cool completely. Serve at room temperature.

You need to take notice when 87-year-old family matriarch Eunice Goldstein bestows her highest praise: "This is a nice little cheesecake, dear." The key is plain and simple: it's all about *really* having the ingredients at room temperature, or between 65°F and 70°F. This means taking the cream cheese out of the refrigerator at least 2 hours before using it. In a hurry? Cut the chilled cream cheese into small pieces and leave it out at room temperature for about 15 minutes. (No cheating with the microwave—it's too risky, since the cream cheese often melts in the middle before softening around the edges.) Take the eggs out of the refrigerator 1 hour before using them, or place them in warm water for about 5 minutes. And last but not least, the sour cream should be at room temperature for 1 hour, or place it in a warm, shallow water bath, stirring frequently, for 15 minutes.

Because the cheesecake needs at least 6 hours to firm in the refrigerator, it is best made a day ahead.

MAKES ONE 8-INCH CAKE, SERVING 8 TO 10

A Nice Little Cheesecake

CRUMB CRUST

1⅓ cups **graham cracker crumbs**

⅓ cup **granulated sugar**

5 tablespoons **unsalted butter,** melted

1. TO MAKE THE CRUMB CRUST: Preheat the oven to 350°F. Place an 8-inch springform pan on a jelly roll pan and set aside.

2. In a medium bowl, mix together the graham cracker crumbs, sugar, and butter until well blended and crumbly. Transfer the mixture to the springform pan and, using the bottom of a measuring cup or your fingertips, lightly press the mixture onto the bottom of the pan. Bake until set and fragrant, about 5 minutes. Transfer to a rack to cool to room temperature.

FILLING

16 ounces **cream cheese,**
at room temperature

¾ cup **granulated sugar**

Pinch of **salt**

1½ teaspoons **pure vanilla extract**

2 **eggs,** at room temperature

TOPPING

8 ounces **sour cream,**
at room temperature

¾ teaspoon **pure vanilla extract**

3. TO MAKE THE FILLING: In a food processor, combine the cream cheese, sugar, salt, and vanilla until creamy and smooth, scraping down the sides and bottom of the bowl as necessary. Incorporate the eggs until fully blended. Pour into the springform pan.

4. Bake in the center of the oven until the top just begins to brown and the center jiggles slightly, 35 to 40 minutes.

5. TO MAKE THE TOPPING: Meanwhile, in a medium bowl, mix together the sour cream and vanilla until blended.

6. Remove the cheesecake from the oven and drop spoonfuls of the topping around the edge of the cake, then gently spread it to cover the cake evenly. Return to the oven and bake for 5 minutes longer. Transfer to a rack to cool completely.

7. Using a paring knife, loosen the sides from the inside edge of the pan. Loosely cover the pan with plastic wrap, and chill the cheesecake for at least 6 hours or overnight. To serve, gently unlatch the sides of the springform pan, and cut the cake into thin wedges. Serve at room temperature. Store, covered loosely with plastic wrap, in the refrigerator for up to 3 days.

If a cake means a celebration, a chocolate cake with a dynamite chocolate frosting means an extra-special one. This delicious cake, based on an old-fashioned Texas sheet cake, is easy to put together. Once the cake is baked and cooled, it takes a few measured cuts to form a dreidel, the four-sided spinning top that's as much a part of Hanukkah as the menorah.

I've used some of the remnant cake pieces to form one of the letters inscribed on the dreidel's four sides—nun, gimel, hay, or shin. They stand for the Hebrew words *"Nes gadol hayah shom,"* or "A great miracle happened there," referring to the olive oil used to rekindle the menorah's flame after the Assyrian army was driven out of Jerusalem and its temple rededicated.

For best results when making this cake, use a straight-edged metal cake pan, not a glass casserole-style baking pan.

MAKES ONE 13-BY-9-INCH CAKE, SERVING 12 TO 14

"Let's Make a Dreidel" Chocolate Cake

CAKE

2 cups **all-purpose flour**

2 cups **granulated sugar**

1 teaspoon **baking soda**

½ teaspoon **salt**

1 cup **unsalted butter**

2 ounces **unsweetened chocolate**

¾ cup **water**

1 teaspoon **instant coffee,** decaffeinated or regular

1. TO MAKE THE CAKE: Preheat the oven to 375°F. Lightly grease a 13-by-9-by-2-inch straight-sided metal cake pan with cooking spray. To help remove the cake, line the pan, lengthwise, with a 17-by-8-inch sheet of parchment paper, and use the overhang as handles. Lightly grease the parchment and set aside.

2. Into a large bowl, sift together the flour, sugar, baking soda, and salt, then lightly whisk and set aside. In a medium saucepan over medium heat, combine the butter, chocolate, water, and instant coffee and bring just to a boil, stirring until smooth. Remove from the heat. Gradually whisk the chocolate mixture into the flour mixture until smooth. Beat in the eggs, buttermilk, and vanilla until smooth, scraping down the sides and bottom of the bowl as necessary. The batter will be thin.

CAKE *continued*

2 **eggs,** lightly beaten

½ cup **buttermilk**

1½ teaspoons **pure vanilla extract**

FROSTING

1 cup **unsalted butter,** preferably a highter-fat European style, at room temperature

4 cups (1 pound) sifted **powdered sugar**

2 ounces **semisweet chocolate,** melted

1 tablespoon **milk** or **half-and-half,** or more if needed

Pinch of **salt**

3. Pour the batter into the prepared pan. Gently tap the pan several times on a counter to settle the batter. Bake until the cake is springy to the touch and a toothpick inserted in the center comes out clean, about 35 minutes. Transfer to a rack to cool for 30 minutes. Use the parchment handles to remove the cake to a flat surface. Cool completely before frosting.

4. TO MAKE THE FROSTING: In a stand mixer set on low speed, beat the butter, powdered sugar, melted chocolate, milk, and salt until the sugar is moist. Slowly increase the speed to medium-high, scraping down the sides and bottom of the bowl as necessary. Beat until it reaches a spreading consistency. If necessary, add more milk for a creamier consistency.

5. TO ASSEMBLE. See the diagram. To form the dreidel's base, using a ruler and a toothpick, measure and mark the 4½-inch center point along one 9-inch side. This becomes the dreidel's spinning point. From both corners of this side, measure up 4 inches on each 13-inch side and mark with a toothpick. Using the toothpicks as a guide, cut out the marked triangles.

6. To form the dreidel's top and spinning knob, using a ruler and a toothpick, measure and mark a 3-inch square in one corner of the remaining 9-inch side. Repeat to measure the other corner. Using the toothpicks as guides, cut out the two marked square corners. The cake remaining in the center forms the knob. Using the remnants, create one of the four Hebrew letters—NUN, GIMEL, HAY, or SHIN—to decorate the top of the cake.

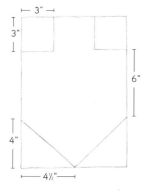

NUN

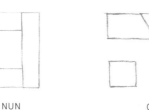
GIMEL

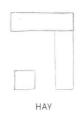
HAY

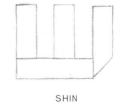
SHIN

7. Place the dreidel cake onto a serving plate. To protect the plate while frosting the cake, place strips of waxed paper under the edges of the cake. Using dollops of frosting, "glue" the Hebrew letter in place before frosting the top and sides of the cake.

DECEMBER

1	2	3	4	5	6	7
8	9	10	11	12	13	14
15	16	17	18	19	20	21
22	23	24	**25**	26	27	28
29	30	31				

Christmas celebrates the birth of the Christ child. It is the most widely celebrated holiday in the world. Though Christmas traditions vary according to country, culture, family, and individual, the spirit of the holiday is unchanging. Christmas is a holy festival to be celebrated and savored with those we love. It is peace on earth, good will toward men. Why Christmas is special to you will depend on the customs handed down in your family from generation to generation. Wonderful food adds to the festivities, and a wealth of old and new traditions come together at the holiday table.

CHRISTMAS

DECEMBER 25

· · · · · · ·

Gingerbread Men and
a Few of Their Holiday Friends 73
Stained Glass Candy Cookie Charms 75
Victorian Scrap Cookies 76

Linzer Wreaths 77

Sofia's Snow Pillows 79

Stir-Up Sunday Fruitcake 80

Saint Lucia's Saffron Crown 82

The Kids' Cinnamon-Roll Christmas Tree 84

Without Thinking Twice Perfect Popovers 87
Hot Chocolate Popovers 88
Gruyère Horseradish Popovers 88

Flashy Cocktail Rings with a Trio of Seeds 89

Christmas Day Trifles for You and Me 90

Snowflake Cake 93
Candy Cane Cupcakes 97

The chubby gingerbread man, thickly cut from a spicy molasses dough, is a classic Christmas cookie. You can't have too many of these friendly fellows, so make a batch or two, using your favorite holiday cookie cutters. It's fun for the kids to decorate their own gingerbread men with raisins or nonmelting candies before baking. Or you can bake undecorated cookies, frost them with ERNA NEUMAN'S ICING (page 47) once they have cooled, and let the kids loose with decorative candies and sugar sprinkles.

To make this recipe your own family original, adjust the spiciness by changing the amount of ginger, cinnamon, cloves, and nutmeg. The choice of light or dark molasses and brown sugar will also be a matter of your individual taste.

MAKES ABOUT 2 DOZEN 5½-INCH COOKIES

Gingerbread Men
and a Few of Their Holiday Friends

2 ¼ cups **all-purpose flour**

¼ teaspoon **baking soda**

½ teaspoon **salt**

2 teaspoons **ground ginger**

1 teaspoon **ground cinnamon**

½ teaspoon **ground cloves**

¼ teaspoon **ground nutmeg**

½ cup **vegetable shortening**

¼ cup firmly packed **light** or **dark brown sugar**

1 **egg**

½ cup **light** or **dark molasses**

1. Into a medium bowl, sift together the flour, baking soda, salt, ginger, cinnamon, cloves, and nutmeg, then lightly whisk and set aside.

2. In a stand mixer set on medium speed, beat the shortening until creamy, about 30 seconds. On medium speed, beat in the brown sugar until light and lump free. Beat in the egg until well blended, scraping down the sides and bottom of the bowl as necessary. Beat in the molasses until blended. Turn off the mixer, add half the flour mixture, and beat on low speed until blended. Add the remaining flour and beat until blended.

3. Using lightly floured hands, gather the sticky dough into a ball. Divide the ball in half and flatten each portion into a 6- to 8-inch disk. Wrap each disk in plastic wrap and chill for 2 hours or until firm.

4. Preheat the oven to 350°F. Line a baking sheet with parchment paper or grease it lightly and set aside.

continued

Gingerbread Men *continued*

5. Remove the dough from the refrigerator and, if needed, soften slightly for easier handling. Roll it out ⅛ inch thick on a lightly floured board, between 2 sheets of parchment paper or heavy-duty plastic wrap, or on a pastry cloth with a cloth-covered rolling pin.

6. Lightly dip a 5½-inch gingerbread man or other Christmas-themed cookie cutter in flour, then firmly press it straight down into the dough. Repeat, cutting the cookies close together to avoid rerolling. Using a spatula, carefully transfer the cookies to the baking sheet. If a cookie is to be used as an ornament, press a hole through the top with a drinking straw or large skewer.

7. Bake until the cookies are lightly browned, 9 to 11 minutes. Let the cookies firm and cool slightly on the baking sheet before transferring to a rack to cool completely. If desired, decorate the cookies with icing and decorative candies.

STAINED GLASS CANDY COOKIE CHARMS

As yummy to eat as they are fun to peek through, these bite-size, candy-filled Christmas cookies look like tiny stained glass windows. When hard candy is crushed and baked in the cut-out center of each cookie, it melts into a translucent sheet of brilliant color. I like to serve these charmlike treats as a sweet surprise at a cocktail party or to use them as a garnish alongside the main dessert.

MAKES UP TO 14 DOZEN COOKIES

Dough for CHOCOLATE GELT HIDE-A-COOKIES (page 48)

Red, green, or yellow hard candy, crushed

1. Follow the CHOCOLATE GELT HIDE-A-COOKIES recipe, setting aside a foil-lined baking sheet and omitting the toilet paper roll. After gathering the dough into a ball, divide the ball in half and flatten each portion into a 6- to 8-inch disk. Roll out the first disk ⅛ inch thick on a lightly floured board, between 2 sheets of parchment paper or heavy-duty plastic wrap, or on a pastry cloth with a cloth-covered rolling pin.

2. Using a small 2- to 2½-inch cookie cutter, cut out the dough and transfer the cookies to a baking sheet. Using a garnish cutter or sharp knife, cut out and remove a major portion of dough from the center of each cookie. Carefully fill the cutouts with red, green, or yellow crushed hard candy.

3. Bake in the center of the oven until the candies melt and the cookies are firm, 5 to 10 minutes, depending on the size (the cut-out dough can also be baked into miniature cookies). Slide the foil off the baking sheet onto a counter, and let the cookies cool completely before gently removing. Repeat with the remaining dough disk.

VICTORIAN SCRAP COOKIES

In Victorian times, sugar cookies, known as "scrap cookies,"
were often decorated with paper illustrations of Saint Nicholas
and other Christmas characters and scenes. You can make
the tradition your own by adding paper decorations to cookies
baked with cut-out spaces. As decorations, use photocopied
photographs of friends and children, or look for Victorian scrap
reproductions in specialty paper shops and import stores.
These cookies make wonderfully old-fashioned tree ornaments,
but they are also meant to be eaten. Remember to remove
the paper decoration before taking a bite.

MAKES 2 TO 4 DOZEN COOKIES, DEPENDING ON SIZE

Dough for GINGERBREAD MEN
AND A FEW OF THEIR HOLIDAY FRIENDS (page 73)

Small paper decorations

"Glue" made of **powdered sugar** mixed with a little **water**

Follow the GINGERBREAD MEN AND A FEW OF THEIR HOLIDAY FRIENDS recipe.
To create small paper decorations to cover the cookies, make stencils using
ovals or squares cut from cardboard to fit the photocopies or reproductions you
have collected. Cut out cookies using the stencils, and bake as directed in the
recipe. (If the cookies are to be used as ornaments, press a hole through the top
with a drinking straw or large skewer.) After the cookies are baked and cooled,
attach the pictures to them with a stiff mixture of powdered sugar and water.
Store the cookies in airtight containers, separated by layers of waxed or parchment paper to prevent the fat in the cookies from staining the pictures.

Cut from traditional linzer dough—a butter-rich hazelnut pastry from Austria—these wreath-shaped cookies will be a tasty hit at your next holiday cookie exchange, and they'll be the prettiest cookies in the lot. The top cookie, dusted with powdered sugar, has a cutout so the black currant preserves are visible. If you want these cookies to look their best, assemble them within a few hours of serving, and arrange them side by side in a single layer to avoid smudging the powdered sugar.

MAKES ABOUT 2 DOZEN 2½-INCH COOKIES

Linzer Wreaths

1½ cups **all-purpose flour**

2 tablespoons **unsweetened cocoa powder**

½ teaspoon **ground cinnamon**

⅛ teaspoon **ground cloves**

¼ teaspoon **salt**

2¼ cups **hazelnut meal** or finely ground **hazelnuts** (see Note)

¾ cup (12 tablespoons) **unsalted butter,** at room temperature

1 cup **granulated sugar**

2 **egg yolks**

1 teaspoon **pure vanilla extract**

Grated zest of 1 small **lemon**

About ½ cup **black currant preserves** or **raspberry jam** or **preserves**

Powdered sugar for dusting

1. Preheat the oven to 375°F. Line a baking sheet with parchment paper or grease it lightly and set aside.

2. Into a medium bowl, sift together the flour, cocoa, cinnamon, cloves, and salt, then lightly whisk in the hazelnuts and set aside.

3. In a stand mixer set on medium speed, beat the butter until creamy, about 30 seconds. Add the sugar and beat until light and fluffy, about 3 minutes. Add the egg yolks and vanilla and beat until fully incorporated, scraping down the sides and bottom of the bowl as necessary. Beat in the lemon zest until blended. Turn off the mixer, add half the flour mixture, and beat on low speed until blended. Add the remaining flour and beat until blended.

4. Use lightly floured hands to gather the sticky dough into a ball. Divide the ball in half and flatten each portion into a 6- to 8-inch disk. Tightly wrap each disk in plastic wrap and chill for 30 minutes. Roll out the first disk ⅛ inch thick on a lightly floured board, between 2 sheets of parchment paper or heavy-duty plastic wrap, or on a pastry cloth with a cloth-covered rolling pin.

continued

Linzer Wreaths *continued*

5. Lightly dip a 2½-inch wreath-shaped cookie cutter or round biscuit cutter in flour, then firmly press it straight down into the dough. Repeat, cutting the cookies close together to avoid rerolling. Using a spatula, carefully transfer the cookies to the baking sheet. Bake until lightly colored, 10 to 12 minutes. Transfer to a rack to cool.

6. Roll out the remaining disk of dough, cut into cookies with the same round cutter, and use a smaller, 1½-inch round garnish cutter to remove the centers from the cookies. Bake the large and small rounds as directed. (The small rounds will take less time to bake, 7 to 9 minutes.) When cool, lightly spread half the large rounds with black currant preserves. Sift powdered sugar onto the cut-out rounds' frames and carefully set them atop the jam-spread rounds. Enjoy the mini-rounds on their own.

NOTE: Hazelnut meal is available in the baking section of many supermarkets or in specialty markets such as Trader Joe's in the nut section. One brand is Bob's Red Mill. Hazelnut meal is finely ground hazelnuts.

Four-year-old Sofia calls these traditional Christmas cookies "snow pillows." Rich with butter and ground pecans, the tender round cookies are generously coated with powdered sugar, so they look like little snow-white cushions. Sofia says they're Santa's favorites, and she should know. Daddy Brian asked her to set out a few for the old gentleman to enjoy last Christmas Eve. In the morning they were all gone, and only a drift of powdered sugar remained. In Greece, these cookies are called *kourabiedes;* in Austria, bakers call them *kipel;* and in Mexico, they are called *bizcochos de boda* and are given as wedding favors.

MAKES ABOUT 2½ DOZEN COOKIES

Sofia's Snow Pillows

1 cup **cake flour**

1 cup **pecan meal** or finely ground **pecans** (see Note)

¼ teaspoon **salt**

½ cup **unsalted butter,** at room temperature

2 cups **powdered sugar,** divided

1 teaspoon **pure vanilla extract**

1. Preheat the oven to 350°F. Line a baking sheet with parchment paper or grease it lightly and set aside.

2. In a bowl, whisk together the flour, pecan meal, and salt until well blended, and set aside.

3. In a medium bowl, beat the butter and ⅓ cup powdered sugar until fluffy. Stir in the vanilla. Gradually add the flour mixture, beating just until the dough clings together. Chill the dough for 20 minutes. Shape the dough into 1-inch balls. Place the cookies about 2 inches apart on the baking sheet. Bake until firm and light brown, about 12 minutes.

4. On a rimmed baking sheet or dish, spread about ½ cup of the remaining powdered sugar. As the tender cookies finish baking, gently transfer 3 or 4 to the sugar-lined dish. Sift or sieve some of the remaining powdered sugar over the warm cookies. Transfer to a rack to cool completely. Repeat with the remaining cookies and powdered sugar.

NOTE: Pecan meal is available in the baking section of some supermarkets. If unavailable, substitute 1 cup whole nuts, ground in a mini-processor as finely as possible without making a paste. Don't worry if the ground nuts aren't completely uniform.

In Oliver Cromwell's 18th-century England, making a fruit-studded, brandy-soaked dessert could land you in jail. Cromwell's strong puritanical faith led him to the conclusion that such desserts were sinfully rich, so he banned them. Luckily for us, public sentiment changed through the years. By the time of Victoria, the fifth Sunday before Christmas was known as Stir-Up Sunday. This was the day when families stirred up their fruitcakes or plum puddings and wrapped them in Cognac-soaked cloths to mellow.

This versatile fruitcake has all your favorite nibbles in one tasty package. You can follow tradition by serving a thin slice for dessert or with tea. Or you can strike out on your own and slip a small serving into your day pack, along with a thermos of hot tea, the next time you go cross-country skiing or take a chilly wintertime hike. I like to call this fruitcake "trail mix with a lift."

MAKES FOUR 6-INCH ROUND CAKES OR FIVE 3-BY-6-INCH MINI-LOAVES

Stir-Up Sunday Fruitcake

1 cup chopped **dried apricots**
plus ¼ cup for garnish

¾ cup chopped **dried cherries**
plus ¼ cup for garnish

1 cup chopped **dried pineapple**

1 cup chopped **dried apples**

½ cup **dried cranberries**

¾ cup **golden raisins**

½ cup **brandy,**
plus more for soaking

1. Preheat the oven to 300°F. Grease four 6-inch springform pans or five 3-by-6-inch mini-loaf pans and set aside.

2. In a large mixing bowl, combine all the dried fruits, except the ones to be used for garnish. Pour the brandy over the fruit, toss to coat, and set aside.

3. In another, larger bowl, whisk together the flour, baking powder, salt, cinnamon, nutmeg, allspice, and cloves until well blended. Stir in the nuts, then the brandy-fruit mixture, and mix until well blended.

1½ cups **all-purpose flour**

1 teaspoon **baking powder**

½ teaspoon **salt**

1 teaspoon **ground cinnamon**

¼ teaspoon **ground nutmeg**

¼ teaspoon **ground allspice**

¼ teaspoon **ground cloves**

1 cup walnut **halves or pieces**

1 cup whole **almonds**

1 cup **pecan halves** or pieces

¾ cup whole **hazelnuts**

2 **eggs,** at room temperature

½ cup **applesauce**

6 tablespoons **unsalted butter,** melted and cooled

¼ cup **light** or **dark molasses**

¾ cup plus 2 tablespoons firmly packed **brown sugar**

4. In a medium bowl, whisk the eggs until frothy. Whisk in the applesauce, butter, and molasses until blended. Stir in the brown sugar and mix until well blended and smooth. Stir the egg mixture into the flour mixture until all the fruits and nuts are coated with batter. Fill the prepared baking pans three quarters full. Garnish the tops with the remaining ¼ cup apricots and the remaining ¼ cup dried cherries by partially pressing the fruit into the batter. Bake for 1 hour. The cakes are done when the sides begin to pull away from the edge of the pan and a toothpick inserted in the middle comes out clean. The cakes will be a rich mahogany color.

5. Cool in the pans for 15 minutes, then turn out onto a rack. When thoroughly cooled, wrap the cakes in cheesecloth that has been soaked in additional brandy. Cover with foil, and store in an airtight container or refrigerator until ready to serve. Allow the cakes to mellow for several weeks. They improve with age (don't we all!).

On December 13, Scandinavian families begin their Christmas celebrations by honoring Saint Lucia. Legends say that in the fourth century, this young Sicilian carried food to persecuted Christians hiding in underground tunnels. To light her way, Lucia wore a wreath of candles on her head.

In many Swedish homes, the Lucia tradition remains. The family's eldest daughter is Lucia for the day. In the morning, she dons a white gown and a candle-lit crown of lingonberry leaves and awakens her parents with a tray of steaming coffee and fragrant golden saffron buns.

In this recipe, the traditional saffron dough is shaped into Saint Lucia's crown. Decorated with small white candles, holly leaves, and berries, it becomes a festive and delectable centerpiece for a Christmas brunch or tea.

MAKES 1 LOAF, SERVING 6 TO 8

Saint Lucia's Saffron Crown

1 cup **milk**

¼ cup plus 2 tablespoons **unsalted butter**

½ cup **granulated sugar**

½ teaspoon **saffron threads**

Pinch of **salt**

4½ teaspoons (about 2 packages) **active dry yeast**

¼ cup **warm water** (110°F to 115°F)

1. In a small saucepan over medium heat, warm the milk and add the butter, sugar, saffron, and salt, stirring until the butter has melted. Transfer to the large bowl of a stand mixer and set aside to cool to lukewarm.

2. In a small bowl, sprinkle the yeast over the warm water, stir to combine, and set aside.

3. Add ¾ cup flour to the milk mixture and mix on low speed until blended, about 1 minute. Beat in the egg yolk on medium speed until well blended, scraping down the sides and bottom of the bowl as necessary. Beat in the yeast mixture until well blended. Gradually stir in enough of the remaining flour, a little at a time, to make a soft dough that pulls away from the sides of the bowl.

3½ cups **all-purpose flour,**
divided

1 **egg,** separated

½ cup **raisins**

½ cup **golden raisins**

⅓ cup chopped **mixed
candied citrus peel**

½ cup **blanched almonds,**
finely chopped

2 tablespoons chopped
blanched almonds

1 to 2 tablespoons **crystal** or
decorative **large-grained sugar**

Small white candles and **holder**
for decorating

Holly leaves and **berries**
for decorating

Room-temperature **butter**
for serving

4. Turn the dough out onto a lightly floured work surface and knead until smooth, satiny, and no longer sticky, 5 to 8 minutes. Knead in the raisins, golden raisins, mixed peel, and finely chopped almonds. Cut the dough into 3 equal pieces. Form each piece into a ball, then roll each one into a 24-inch length. Lay the 3 lengths of dough, side by side, on a lightly oiled baking sheet. Start braiding the lengths of dough loosely from the center to the ends. Loop the braided dough into a ring, join the ends, and pinch together. Cover the braid and let rise in a warm place for 1 hour.

5. Preheat the oven to 375°F.

6. Lightly beat the egg white and brush the ring with it. Sprinkle with the chopped blanched almonds and sugar. Bake until the top is golden brown and the bread sounds hollow, about 25 minutes. Check the bread at 20 minutes and cover with foil if it starts to over-brown. Transfer to a rack to cool slightly. Decorate with small white candles and holders, holly leaves, and berries. Serve warm with softened butter.

You can take it from me and my eight-year-old sidekick Dylan: These biscuit-like rolls, baked in the shape of a Christmas tree, are a treat for adults as well as kids, and they're a cinch to make. The store-bought mix makes them quick to fix. And the ingredients you put in the filling make them delicious (no skimping allowed here). Let your favorite forest elves help to measure the ingredients and mix the dough. Once the rolls are baked and iced, your helpers may want to decorate the tree with green crystal sugar and red jelly ornaments.

MAKES 16 ROLLS

The Kids' Cinnamon-Roll Christmas Tree

ROLLS

2½ cups **biscuit mix,** preferably Bisquick

¼ cup **granulated sugar**

⅔ cup **whole milk**

FILLING

¼ cup **unsalted butter,** melted

¼ cup plus 2 tablespoons **granulated sugar**

1¼ teaspoons **ground cinnamon**

¼ cup finely chopped **walnuts**

1. Preheat the oven to 400°F. Line a baking sheet with parchment paper.

2. TO MAKE THE ROLLS: In a large mixing bowl, whisk together the biscuit mix and sugar until well blended. Stir in the milk until a soft dough forms. If the dough is too sticky, add more biscuit mix, 1 tablespoon at a time, until it is easy to handle. Turn the dough out onto a lightly floured board or pastry cloth and knead gently about 10 times. Roll into a 16-by-9-inch rectangle.

3. TO FILL THE ROLLS: Spread the dough with the melted butter. Mix together the sugar and cinnamon. Sprinkle the cinnamon sugar over the buttered dough. Spread, if necessary, so that no dry sugar remains and the mixture is evenly distributed. Sprinkle the nuts over the cinnamon sugar. Starting with a long side, roll the dough up jelly roll fashion, and pinch the edges together to seal. Cut into sixteen 1-inch slices.

GLAZE

3 tablespoons **unsalted butter,** melted

1 cup **powdered sugar**

½ teaspoon **pure vanilla extract**

1 to 2 tablespoons **hot water**

Green crystal sugar
for decorating (optional)

Red jelly
for decorating (optional)

4. TO FORM THE TREE: To form the trunk, center a first roll near the bottom of the baking sheet. To form the base of the tree, place 5 rolls side by side in a line, centered over the trunk. Leave ½ inch between all the rolls, and put the seam side inward. Place 4 rolls, side by side, above the first row. Top with a 3-roll row, then a 2-roll row, and finally a 1-roll row.

5. Bake until golden brown, 12 to 15 minutes. Slip the parchment paper with the rolls onto a flat surface and let the rolls cool slightly before glazing (to keep the glaze from running).

6. TO MAKE THE GLAZE: In a medium bowl, mix the melted butter, powdered sugar, and vanilla. Stir in the hot water, 1 tablespoon at a time, until the glaze is slightly runny. Spread over the slightly cooled rolls and serve. If desired, decorate by sprinkling the glaze with green sugar crystals, and to make red ornaments, randomly place small dollops of red jelly between the rows.

Practice this recipe once, and without thinking twice, you'll master it. These golden, crispy, lighter-than-air popovers make an elegant dinner even grander, turn leftover meals into special occasions, and make any breakfast a holiday when they're smeared with butter and homemade jam.

It's crucial to follow the recipe, making sure that all your ingredients are at room temperature. The first time you make the popovers, watch the time and discover the nuances of your own oven's temperature. My oven stays at a constant 400°F, while my neighbor's doesn't, so he preheats his to 425°F and then lowers it to 400°F after 5 minutes, giving the popovers the necessary initial blast of heat.

While a popover pan may seem like an extravagant purchase, I highly recommend it. The shape and depth of the cups creates a dramatic pouf on top that makes a spectacular presentation. You can also use deep ironstone custard cups for these popovers, but shy away from shallow muffin tins.

MAKES 6 POPOVERS

Without Thinking Twice Perfect Popovers

6 teaspoons **unsalted butter**

2 **eggs,** lightly beaten, at room temperature

1 cup **milk,** at room temperature

1 cup **all-purpose flour**

½ teaspoon **salt**

1. Preheat the oven to 400°F for 20 minutes. Lightly coat the bottom and sides of six popover-tin cups (or six ½-cup custard cups) with 1 teaspoon butter each. Place the popover pan on a baking sheet.

2. In a small bowl, lightly whisk the eggs until they change color. Whisk in the milk.

3. In a medium bowl, whisk together the flour and salt until well blended. Gently whisk the egg mixture into the flour mixture until only small lumps are left, and set aside.

continued

Perfect Popovers *continued*

4. Place the prepared popover tin and baking sheet in the oven for 4 minutes. At 3 minutes, pour the batter into a lipped pitcher or bowl and lightly whisk. Using an oven mitt, remove the hot popover tin from the oven and immediately divide the batter among the prepared cups. Bake for 23 minutes without opening the oven door. The popovers will be puffy, with crisp brown crusts and hollow, moist interiors. Serve immediately. (For next time, be sure to note the oven time that works for you.)

• • •

VARIATIONS

Children will love Hot Chocolate Popovers for breakfast with fresh fruit and a drizzle of maple syrup, or you could serve them as a dessert with a scoop of ice cream and some rich fudge sauce. Follow the main recipe, decreasing the flour to ¾ teaspoon plus 2 tablespoons and adding ¼ cup **unsweetened Dutch process cocoa powder** to the dry ingredients. Proceed as directed.

For a snappy accompaniment to a Christmas Eve prime rib roast, try Gruyère Horseradish Popovers. Follow the main recipe. Before whisking the flour mixture into the egg mixture, stir in 2 tablespoons prepared **horseradish.** When the batter is smooth, stir in ½ cup finely grated **Gruyère cheese,** and proceed as directed.

Add these crackery snacks to your Christmas Eve cocktail menu, and set out a few for Santa Claus. He'll have a hard time leaving for his appointed rounds. Cheesy, buttery, and delectable, they're also chic and handsome, whether dressed in black and white sesame seeds, shiny black onion seeds, or a rainbow blend of cracked peppercorns. If any are left, they'll go very well with a soup or salad.

MAKES 2 DOZEN RINGS

Flashy Cocktail Rings with a Trio of Seeds

Dough for the GOLDEN SAVORY CHEESE COINS (page 65), omitting the turmeric and water

1 **egg,** lightly beaten

TOPPING
(choose one of the following)

½ cup **mixed black and white sesame seeds**

½ cup **black onion seeds** (see Note)

½ cup **medium-coarse cracked black pepper** or **rainbow pepper blend,** such as Szechuan

1. Prepare the dough as instructed in the recipe. After transferring the flour mixture from the bowl into a resealable plastic bag, push the dough together until blended. Using clean fingers, divide the dough into 24 pieces.

2. Roll each piece into a 5-inch strip, pinching and smoothing the ends together. Brush the top and sides with the beaten egg, and roll the tops and sides in the topping of your choice. Bake as directed and serve at room temperature.

NOTE: Black onion seeds are available at Middle Eastern grocery stores or specialty shops.

No two cooks see eye to eye on how to prepare a Christmas trifle, a parfait-like confection that everyone seems to love. Yet everyone agrees that a trifle is one of the most elegant and delicious ways to end a holiday meal. Here's a recipe you can enjoy, adapt, and make your very own.

SERVES 8

Christmas Day Trifles for You and Me

PASTRY CREAM

2 cups **half-and-half**

4 **egg yolks**

¼ cup **granulated sugar**

2 tablespoons **all-purpose flour**

½ teaspoon **pure vanilla extract**

FILLING

16 teaspoons good, **dry sherry**

8 **slightly stale** or **dry slices** "SHALL I BE MOTHER?" TEATIME POUND CAKE (page 112) or purchased **pound cake,** cut into ¾-inch slices

1 jar (at least 16 ounces) best possible **raspberry preserves,** strained through a fine sieve

8 to 10 **amaretti cookies** (Italian macaroons)

continued

1. TO MAKE THE PASTRY CREAM: In a heavy, medium saucepan over medium-high heat, bring the half-and-half to a boil. Meanwhile, in a medium bowl, whisk together the egg yolks and sugar until smooth, pale yellow, and thick, about 1 minute. Whisk in the flour. Slowly whisk the boiling half-and-half into the egg mixture until blended, then pour the mixture back into the saucepan and cook over medium-high heat, whisking constantly, until the pastry cream thickens and boils, about 6 minutes. Remove from the heat and stir in the vanilla. Transfer to a clean bowl and press plastic wrap onto the surface. Chill for at least 6 hours or up to 2 days. Makes about 2 cups.

2. TO MAKE THE FILLING: Drizzle 1 teaspoon of the sherry on one side of each slice of cake (it is quickly absorbed). Flip, drizzle the other sides with another 1 teaspoon sherry each, then spread each with 1 tablespoon of the raspberry preserves. Set the remaining preserves aside. Remove the crusts, if desired, and cut the prepared cake slices into bite-size cubes. Set aside. Crush the amaretti cookies and set aside. (If the cookies come individually wrapped, crush them in their wrapping. That way, they're already measured for each trifle.)

continued

Christmas Day Trifles *continued*

TOPPING

1 cup **heavy (whipping) cream**

2 tablespoons **granulated sugar**

1 tablespoon **good, dry sherry**

4 **amaretti cookies,** finely crushed, for garnishing

3. TO MAKE THE TOPPING: In a chilled bowl, beat together the cream and sugar. As the cream begins to thicken, gradually drizzle in the sherry. Continue beating until the cream is softly to moderately whipped.

4. TO ASSEMBLE: Arrange eight 8- to 10-ounce clear goblets on a work surface. Spoon 1 teaspoon of the remaining raspberry preserves into each goblet, followed by a spoonful of pastry cream. Next, divide half of the cake cubes among the goblets, arranging them preserves side out. Top each with 1 generous tablespoon pastry cream, drizzle 1 teaspoon preserves over the pastry cream, and sprinkle with half of the crushed amaretti. Repeat, layering the pound cake, pastry cream, preserves, and amaretti one more time. Top each trifle with the whipped cream. Garnish with a dusting of the amaretti crumbs and a drizzle of preserves, if desired. Chill for at least 1 hour, or until serving time. The finished trifle will keep, refrigerated, for 3 hours.

To my way of thinking, behind every memorable holiday meal, there's a great cake—the kind that looks so grand and tastes so great that it becomes an instant tradition. Look no further, because you've found it.

Since this is a made-from-scratch cake, you'll need to plan ahead. I like to make the cake the night before. For decorating, I've suggested a drift of white chocolate snowflakes to cover the snowy frosting, but there are easier ways to top this charmer. Why not let the kids decorate it with toy skiers, skaters, or snowboarders? How about a few green gumdrop trees and a family of marshmallow snowmen?

You'll notice that this simple frosting is made primarily from butter, and for this recipe I highly recommend using a European-style, high-fat butter such as Plugra (82 percent fat), Land O' Lakes Ultra Creamy (83 percent fat), or another artisan-style organic butter with a fat content above the normal 80 percent. European butters are cultured like yogurt or cheese, giving them a richer, deeper flavor. The added fat carries more of the vanilla flavoring to the mouth and contributes to a silkier texture.

MAKES ONE 9-INCH LAYER CAKE, SERVING 14 TO 16

Snowflake Cake

CAKE

3 cups **cake flour**

2 teaspoons **baking soda**

¾ teaspoon **salt**

continued

1. Preheat the oven to 350°F. Grease and flour two 9-inch cake pans. Line the bottom of each pan with waxed or parchment paper. Grease and flour the top side of the paper, and set aside.

2. TO MAKE THE CAKE: Into a medium bowl, sift together the flour, baking soda, and salt, then lightly whisk and set aside.

continued

Snowflake Cake *continued*

CAKE *continued*

¾ cup plus 2 tablespoons **unsalted butter,** at room temperature

2½ cups **granulated sugar**

3 **eggs,** separated while cold, at room temperature

1 tablespoon **pure vanilla extract**

2 cups **buttermilk**

continued

3. In a stand mixer set on medium speed, beat the butter until creamy, about 30 seconds. Add the sugar and beat until light and nearly white, about 5 minutes. Add the egg yolks, one at a time, and beat until fully incorporated, scraping down the sides and bottom of the bowl as necessary. Beat in the vanilla until blended. Add the flour mixture, alternating with the buttermilk, in several additions, and beat until smooth and just blended. Scrape the sides and bottom.

4. In another bowl, beat the egg whites until stiff peaks just form. Gently stir one third of the whites into the batter to lighten it. Fold in the remaining egg whites until just incorporated and no large white streaks of egg white remain.

5. Divide the batter between the prepared pans, using a spatula to evenly spread the batter. Gently rotate the pans to settle and level the batter. Bake until the cakes begin to pull away from the sides and a toothpick inserted in the center comes out clean, about 35 minutes. Let the layers cool in their pans. Gently loosen the edges with a thin knife before inverting the layers onto wire racks. Let the cakes cool thoroughly before carefully peeling off the paper. Cool completely before frosting, about 3 hours.

continued

Snowflake Cake *continued*

SNOWFLAKES

1½ (3-ounce) **white chocolate candy bars**

Silver dragées
for decorating (optional)

FROSTING

1 cup **unsalted butter,**
preferably a high-fat European style, at room temperature

4 cups (1 pound) sifted **powdered sugar**

1 tablespoon **pure vanilla extract**

1 tablespoon **milk** or **half-and-half**

Pinch of **salt**

6. TO MAKE THE SNOWFLAKES: Line a baking sheet with foil. Put the chocolate into a resealable plastic bag and immerse the bag in hot water until the chocolate melts. Dry the bag, then snip off a small piece from one corner. Pipe as many 2-inch snowflakes onto the foil as possible, and decorate the points with silver dragées, if desired. Place the sheet of snowflakes in the freezer until the cake is ready to decorate.

7. TO MAKE THE FROSTING: In a stand mixer set on low speed, beat the butter, powdered sugar, vanilla, milk, and salt until the sugar is moist. Slowly increase the speed to medium-high, scraping down the sides and bottom of the bowl as necessary. Beat until light and creamy, about 1½ minutes.

8. TO ASSEMBLE THE CAKE: Place a dollop of frosting in the middle of the serving platter. Place the bottom layer of the cake on the platter, top side down. Using a narrow metal spatula, spread a third of the frosting over the bottom layer. Place the remaining layer on top. Spread the rest of the frosting over the top and sides of the cake. Remove the snowflakes from the freezer and gently peel off the foil. Be careful—these flakes are fragile. (Don't worry if some of the tips break or chip; in a snow flurry, they'll still look good.) Cover the top and sides of the cake with snowflakes.

9. Chill the cake for an hour to set the frosting and snowflakes. If you are serving the cake on the day it is made, keep it at a cool room temperature after chilling. To cut, use a sharp, thin-bladed knife. Dip the knife into hot water before cutting to prevent the frosting from sticking. Insert the point of the knife into the cake's center. Cut, using an up-and-down motion, pulling the knife toward you.

continued

• • •

VARIATION

Cupcakes are easy to eat, easy to make, and easy to serve to a crowd. Make these Candy Cane Cupcakes for your next party or potluck and watch them disappear faster than a snowflake. Follow the main recipe, lining standard muffin cups (about 30 cups, or bake the cupcakes in batches) with **foil** or **paper liners.** Bake until the cupcake tops are pale gold and a toothpick inserted in the center comes out clean, 20 to 24 minutes. Makes about 30 cupcakes.

For the cupcake frosting, follow the main frosting recipe, substituting ½ teaspoon **pure peppermint extract** and 2½ teaspoons **vanilla** for the 1 tablespoon pure vanilla extract. Immediately after frosting the cupcakes, sprinkle the frosting with coarsely crushed **candy canes** (you'll need about 6 large candy canes).

On December 26, if you live in the United States, you are probably in the midst of the day-after-Christmas cleanup let-down. But if you're Canadian or if you live in any part of the British Commonwealth, the holiday razzmatazz is still in full force, with late-morning brunches, afternoon teas, a cricket game or soccer match, and opportunities to volunteer your time for those who are less fortunate. That's because the day after Christmas is an official holiday called Boxing Day.

DECEMBER

1	2	3	4	5	6	7
8	9	10	11	12	13	14
15	16	17	18	19	20	21
22	23	24	25	**26**	27	28
29	30	31				

It's rooted in Victorian England, where it was the custom for employers to fill small boxes with money as a Yuletide tip for servants and tradespeople. These boxes, or "banks," were made of metal or pottery, with slits in the top that made it easy for people to drop in gifts of money (now you know the origin of the piggy bank, too). Boxing Day was also the time when church collection boxes were opened and the money was distributed to the poor.

BOXING DAY

DECEMBER 26

· · · · · · ·

Buckingham Palace Shortbread 100

Boxing Day Scones with Warm Strawberry Jam 103

The Amazing Leftover Eggnog
and Cinnamon Roll Bread Pudding 104
Jamberry Maple Syrup 105

Sweet Onion, Apple, and Cheese Tart 106

Chip-Shot Pizza with Black Forest Ham,
Smoked Gouda, and Apricot Mustard 108

Stilton Pinwheels with Walnuts and Honey 111

"Shall I Be Mother?" Teatime Pound Cake 112

La Galette des Rois 114

I love shortbread. I love to eat it, I love to make it, and I love to give it away. If you stop by my house on the day after Christmas, more than likely I'll be baking a batch of Buckingham Palace Shortbread, a recipe given to me by Oregon tea maven, Jan Lambert. She insists that it's the very recipe made daily for the Queen's afternoon tea. The secret to its superfine texture is the combination of cake flour and cornstarch. If you're a dough taster, resist the temptation. The sweet, buttery goodness doesn't come through until the fine sugar crowns the just–baked shortbread.

MAKES 2 TO 3 DOZEN 1- TO 1½-INCH SQUARES

Buckingham Palace Shortbread

2 cups **cake flour**

¾ cup plus 1 tablespoon **cornstarch**

¼ teaspoon **salt**

1 cup **unsalted butter,** at room temperature

⅓ cup **granulated sugar**

Up to ¼ cup **baker's** or **superfine sugar** for sprinkling (see Note)

1. In a medium bowl, whisk together the flour, cornstarch, and salt until well blended.

2. In a stand mixer set on medium speed, beat the butter until creamy. Beat in the granulated sugar until light and fluffy, about 2 minutes, scraping down the sides and bottom of the bowl as necessary. On low speed, add the flour mixture in two or three additions until it forms a soft dough. Wrap the dough with plastic wrap and chill for 30 minutes.

3. Preheat the oven to 350°F. Line a baking sheet with parchment paper or leave ungreased.

4. On a lightly floured surface, roll the dough out to a ¾-inch-thick slab, about 5 by 8 inches. (I use a kitchen ruler to measure and press the edges into shape.) Transfer to the baking sheet and bake until lightly golden and firm to the touch, about 40 minutes. Slip the parchment paper with the shortbread onto a hard surface. Immediately sprinkle the shortbread heavily with the baker's sugar. While still warm, use the ruler and a paring knife, pointed straight down, to cut the shortbread into 1- or 1½-inch pieces. Let cool completely. The shortbread tastes best at room temperature.

NOTE: Baker's sugar is available in supermarket baking sections. For a quick substitute, whirl granulated sugar in a blender until fine, about 20 seconds.

Now that you're through making your lists and checking them twice, and the reindeer have come and gone, it's your turn to settle down for a long—and much-deserved—winter's break. Use it to nap, watch an old movie, or enjoy what quite possibly could be the world's best-tasting scone. In the wink of an eye, with the stir of a spoon, these flaky, tender, buttery buttermilk scones will put you to rights in no time at all.

MAKES 16 SCONES

Boxing Day Scones with Warm Strawberry Jam

3 cups **all-purpose flour**

⅓ cup **granulated sugar**

2½ teaspoons **baking powder**

½ teaspoon **baking soda**

¾ teaspoon **salt**

¾ cup cold **unsalted butter,** cut into small pieces

1 cup **buttermilk**

Strawberry jam, homemade or purchased, slightly warmed, for serving

1. Preheat the oven to 400°F. Line a baking sheet with parchment paper or grease it lightly and set aside.

2. Into a large bowl, sift together the flour, sugar, baking powder, baking soda, and salt, then lightly whisk. Use a pastry blender, 2 knives, or your fingers to cut or work the butter into the flour mixture until it resembles fine crumbs.

3. Make a well in the center of the flour-butter mixture, and add the buttermilk all at once. Stir the mixture until the dough pulls away from the sides of the bowl. Using lightly floured hands, gather the dough into a soft ball and turn it out onto a lightly floured work surface. Divide into 4 parts and pat each one into a ¾-inch-thick circle. Cut each circle into 4 wedges.

4. Transfer the wedges to the prepared baking sheet, and bake in the center of the oven until the scones rise and are golden brown, 12 to 15 minutes. Remove and cool for 5 minutes on the baking sheet, then transfer to a rack. Serve warm, split and spread with warm strawberry jam. The scones are best eaten within several hours of baking.

How can it be that the best breakfast of the holiday season relies completely on leftovers? Don't try to figure it out, but make sure that you've stocked up on the required goodies. This wonderful twist on a classic bread pudding takes advantage of the sweet affinity between a favorite holiday beverage and a much-loved breakfast food.

SERVES 6 TO 8

The Amazing Leftover Eggnog and Cinnamon Roll Bread Pudding

4 to 6 large **cinnamon rolls** or other sweet yeast rolls or bread, preferably a day or two old

3 **eggs**

1¼ cups **whole-milk eggnog,** purchased or homemade

1¼ cups **heavy (whipping) cream**

Powdered sugar for dusting

WARM JAMBERRY MAPLE SYRUP (facing page) or **warm maple syrup** for serving (optional)

1. Cut the cinnamon rolls into 1-inch cubes to equal 8 cups. (You can do this several days ahead and leave the cubes out to dry further or store them in containers until needed.)

2. THE NIGHT BEFORE: Butter a shallow, 2½-quart baking dish and distribute the cubes evenly in the dish. Portions of the cubes may be higher than the side of the dish.

3. In a medium bowl, lightly whisk the eggs. Whisk in the eggnog and cream until blended and no yolk shows. Carefully pour three quarters of the egg mixture over the cubes, and use the back of a spoon or your fingers to press the cubes into the liquid. Let rest for 10 minutes to allow the cubes to soak up the custard, then pour in the remaining egg mixture. Make sure that every cube is saturated. Cover the dish with plastic wrap or foil and refrigerate overnight. (To assemble in the morning, follow the procedure just described, but let the cubes rest in the egg mixture for a total of 30 minutes before baking.)

4. ABOUT AN HOUR BEFORE SERVING: Preheat the oven to 350°F.

5. Remove the plastic wrap and place the uncovered dish in a large roasting pan. Fill the pan with enough hot water to come halfway up the sides of the dish. Bake in the center of the oven until the cubes are toasted and the pudding is set around the edges, about 50 minutes. Remove the dish from the water as soon as you remove it from the oven. Transfer to a rack to cool for 10 minutes. Dust with powdered sugar. To serve, scoop out portions and serve plain, or accompany with JAMBERRY MAPLE SYRUP or warm maple syrup.

JAMBERRY MAPLE SYRUP

With its hint of orange zest, this medley of cranberries and blueberries makes a delicious alternative to plain maple syrup.

MAKES ABOUT 2 CUPS

¾ cup **cranberries**

½ teaspoon minced **orange zest**

1 cup **pure maple syrup**

½ cup **frozen** or **fresh blueberries**

In a small saucepan over medium-low heat, combine the cranberries, orange zest, and maple syrup. Bring to a simmer and cook for 7 minutes. Add the blueberries, and continue to cook until they begin to burst, 3 to 5 minutes longer. Pour into a pitcher and serve warm. Place any leftover syrup in a covered container in the refrigerator for up to 3 weeks; reheat gently before serving.

Here is a tart that plays its part, morning, noon, and night. It can be the star attraction at breakfast, play a leading role at brunch, or be an immensely satisfying supporting performer at a suppertime buffet. If there are any leftovers, you can rewarm slices or serve them at room temperature, and the crowd will be glad for the encore.

MAKES ONE 9-INCH TART, SERVING 6

Sweet Onion, Apple, and Cheese Tart

FLAKY PASTRY CRUST (page 25)

2 tablespoons **unsalted butter,** divided

2 small **Granny Smith** or **Newtown Pippin apples,** peeled, cored, and cut into ⅛-inch lengthwise slices, divided

2 medium **red onions,** thinly sliced

1 teaspoon **granulated sugar**

½ teaspoon **dried thyme**

2 **eggs,** at room temperature

1 cup **half-and-half** or **heavy (whipping) cream**

½ teaspoon **salt**

Freshly ground **black pepper**

½ cup crumbled **blue cheese**

1 cup plus 2 tablespoons **grated cheddar cheese,** divided

1. Follow the directions for preparing and baking the crust, substituting a 9-inch round or fluted tart pan with removable bottom for the 9-inch pie pan. Keep the oven set at 375°F.

2. Meanwhile, in a large skillet over medium-high heat, melt 1 tablespoon butter and sauté half the apple slices until they are tender and beginning to brown, 3 to 4 minutes. Transfer to the tart shell and arrange in a single layer.

3. In the same skillet over medium-high heat, melt the remaining 1 tablespoon butter and sauté the onions until very soft and golden, about 10 minutes. Add the sugar and thyme and continue to sauté until the onions are lightly caramelized and any liquid has evaporated, 1 to 2 minutes. Remove from the heat and let the onions cool slightly.

4. Meanwhile, in a medium bowl, whisk together the eggs, cream, salt, and a couple of grinds of pepper until blended. Stir in the blue cheese, 1 cup cheddar cheese, and the onions.

5. Place the prepared tart pan on a baking sheet. Pour the mixture into the tart shell. It will be very full. Arrange the remaining apple slices in a decorative circular pattern around the top, and sprinkle with the remaining 2 tablespoons cheddar cheese.

6. Bake until the top is golden brown and a knife inserted in the center comes out clean, 35 to 45 minutes. Transfer to a rack to cool for 5 to 10 minutes. Serve warm or at room temperature.

Nowadays, anyone who has frozen pizza or bread dough stashed in the freezer can be a pro on the pizza circuit. Here is my current favorite, and one that I like to serve casually, at the last minute. The pizza is spirited, yet as comforting as Dad's favorite ham and cheese sandwich.

Instead of a pizza sauce base, I like to spread a layer of my favorite olive oil, then arrange overlapping slices of smoky Black Forest ham and semisoft Gouda cheese. After this has baked and the cheese has melted, I add fresh green onions, as many as I can handle, and golden mounds of sweet yet tangy apricot mustard. Add a dash or a drizzle of star anise syrup, and you'll find there's no way you'll share a bite with anyone else at the table.

My inspiration and thanks for this dish go to Indonesian chef Richard van Rossum, who redefines the Philippine and Dutch dishes of his childhood with enough style to make even a timid diner feel adventurous.

SERVES 4 TO 6

Chip-Shot Pizza with Black Forest Ham, Smoked Gouda, and Apricot Mustard

APRICOT MUSTARD

½ cup **orange juice**

½ cup **cider vinegar** or **rice vinegar**

1½ tablespoons **dry mustard powder**

½ teaspoon **ground coriander**

1. TO MAKE THE MUSTARD: In a bowl, mix together the orange juice, vinegar, dry mustard, and ground coriander until blended. Stir in the mustard seeds and apricots until combined. Season to taste with salt and pepper. If needed, stir in a little water so that the mixture is a bit soupy. Cover and set aside or refrigerate overnight (the apricots will absorb the water). Makes about 2 cups.

1 tablespoon **mustard seeds**

2 cups loosely packed
dried apricots, finely chopped

Salt and freshly ground
black pepper

Water as needed

SYRUP

½ cup **molasses**

1 cup **light corn syrup**

1 tablespoon **cardamom pods**

2 **cinnamon sticks**

1 tablespoon **star anise** (about 6)

PIZZA

8 ounces **frozen pizza** or
bread dough, thawed

Extra-virgin olive oil
for brushing crust

6 slices Black Forest ham
(1 ounce each)

16 ounces **smoked Gouda**
cheese, grated or sliced

4 **green onions,** tender green
and some white parts, chopped

2. TO MAKE THE SYRUP: In a saucepan over low heat, stir together the molasses and corn syrup. Meanwhile, in a dry skillet over medium heat, toast the cardamom pods, cinnamon sticks, and star anise until fragrant, 3 to 4 minutes. Transfer the spices to the molasses mixture and continue to cook until the syrup begins to foam, about 10 minutes. Set aside to cool. The syrup can be made ahead and stored indefinitely. Let the spices remain in the syrup; they can be removed for serving. Makes about 1½ cups.

3. TO MAKE THE PIZZA: Preheat the oven to 425°F. Dust and prepare a pizza stone according to the manufacturer's instructions, or dust a baking sheet with cornmeal and set aside.

4. Place the dough on a lightly floured surface and dust with flour. Press the dough into a circle, then roll it out with a lightly floured rolling pin until it is about ¼ inch thick, keeping the edges thicker than the center. Roll the edges over to create a thin lip. Lay the round of dough on the prepared stone or sheet. Chill for 30 minutes.

5. Remove the crust from the refrigerator and brush the top as well as the edges with olive oil, then overlap the ham slices on top, leaving a ½-inch border around the edges. Top with the cheese. Bake in the lower third of the oven until the crust is crisp and the cheese is bubbly, 10 to 12 minutes. Sprinkle with green onions, slice, garnish with apricot mustard, and serve immediately. Pass the syrup for drizzling over each slice.

Whether for an elegant holiday dinner party or a casual post–Christmas meal with friends, if you want to entertain a crowd without a lot of work and get *oohs* and *aahs* in the process, serve these tasty appetizers. Remember, first impressions are the lasting ones.

MAKES ABOUT 6 DOZEN PINWHEELS

Stilton Pinwheels with Walnuts and Honey

⅓ cup (2¾ ounces) **Stilton** or other **blue cheese,** at room temperature

¼ cup **cream cheese,** at room temperature

1 sheet purchased **frozen puff pastry,** thawed

2 cups (about 8 ounces) **walnut halves,** picked over

Honey for drizzling

1. In a mini-processor or by hand, mix together the cheese and cream cheese until blended.

2. On a lightly floured pastry cloth or board, unfold the pastry sheet according to the package directions. Cut in half lengthwise.

3. Carefully spread half of the cheese mixture to cover one piece of pastry, but leaving a ¼-inch border on one long edge. Beginning with the long coated edge, tightly roll the pastry, forming a long jelly roll–style log. Moisten the border with water and pinch the edge to form a secure seam. Wrap in plastic wrap and freeze for 1 hour or until ready to bake. Repeat with the remaining piece of pastry and cheese mixture.

4. Preheat the oven to 400°F. Line a baking sheet with parchment paper or leave ungreased and set aside.

5. Remove one log at a time from the freezer and unwrap on a cutting board. Thaw slightly. Measure and mark ¼-inch increments and slice with a serrated knife. Arrange the pinwheels on the baking sheet, at least 1 inch apart. Gently press 1 walnut half into the center of each pinwheel. Bake until the pastry is golden brown, 10 to 12 minutes. Remove from the oven and, using a teaspoon or squeeze bottle, drizzle with a crisscross thread of honey. Serve immediately.

The proprietress noticed two women sitting at the sun-dappled table overlooking the lake. They were visitors to Nelson, B.C., and had stopped by her tea shoppe for pound cake and tea. They hesitated, deciding who would serve the just-brewed pot. So she approached.

"Shall I be Mother?" she offered, and went on to pour the first cup. The women smiled as she explained the phrase derived from Victorian custom. Then she went to look after her other guests, leaving the women to sip and to savor their good fortune.

Another time-honored pleasure is making a classic pound cake from scratch. Its buttery flavor is beyond compare. In the absence of chemical leaveners, the crumb and the texture rely on the air incorporated into the batter through beating, the power of the egg whites, and the fortitude of the baker who patiently combines them. Every bite brings the reward.

MAKES 1 LOAF, SERVING 12

"Shall I Be Mother?" Teatime Pound Cake

1. Preheat the oven to 350°F. Lightly coat the bottom and sides of a 9-by-5-inch loaf pan (7½-cup capacity) with cooking spray and set aside.

2. In a small bowl, whisk together the 3 whole eggs, the 3 egg yolks, and the vanilla until well blended.

3. Use a stand mixer on medium speed to beat the butter and 1 cup sugar until the mixture is light, fluffy, and nearly white, about 5 minutes. Add the yolk mixture, a soup spoon full at a time, until it is blended. Periodically turn off the mixer and scrape down the sides and bottom of the bowl. Adding the yolk mixture in this way will take 7 to 10 minutes. It is important to do so very slowly so that the batter does not curdle. (If the batter does curdle, continue as directed. The cake will still be tasty, though its texture and crumb will be less than perfect.)

6 **eggs,** at room temperature, 3 separated while cold

1½ teaspoons **pure vanilla extract**

1 cup **unsalted butter,** at room temperature

1⅓ cups **granulated sugar,** divided

1¾ cups **cake flour**

½ teaspoon **salt**

4. In a medium bowl, whisk together the flour and salt. Sift the flour mixture, ½ cup at a time, into the butter mixture. Using a rubber spatula, gently fold in each addition just until no dry flour appears, scraping up from the bottom of the bowl.

5. In a stand mixer on medium-low speed, beat the 3 egg whites until frothy, about 30 seconds. Raise the speed to medium-high and gradually add the remaining ⅓ cup sugar. Beat on high speed until soft peaks form.

6. Gently fold one-quarter of the beaten egg whites into the flour mixture to lighten it. Fold in the remaining egg whites until just incorporated and no large streaks of egg white remain.

7. Scrape the batter into the prepared pan, smoothing the top. Bake until a toothpick inserted into the middle comes out clean, 50 to 60 minutes. Let the cake cool in the pan for 5 minutes, then transfer to a rack to cool to room temperature.

During the French holidays, you'll spot this "cake of kings" in every small pastry shop and bakery. The lovely puff pastry, filled with a sweet almond frangipane and easily made with frozen dough from the supermarket, celebrates the three kings' visit to the baby Jesus in Bethlehem.

Many French families celebrate this visit on January 6, the Feast of the Epiphany, when they serve the cake with great fanfare. The secret ingredient is a flat, dried bean, or *feve*. One tradition calls for the youngest child in the family to hide under the dining room table and announce which guest each slice of cake should be given to. The person who finds the hidden bean becomes king or queen for the day and wears a golden paper crown. With or without a coronation, this regal pastry will add the crowning touch to your holiday entertaining.

MAKES ONE 9-INCH CAKE, SERVING 6 TO 8

La Galette des Rois

FILLING

¾ cup **almond meal** (see Note)

⅓ cup **granulated sugar**

⅛ teaspoon **salt**

1 **egg**

1 to 2 teaspoons **cherry, pear, or raspberry brandy** (optional)

3 tablespoons **unsalted butter,** at room temperature

1. TO MAKE THE FILLING: In a medium bowl, mix together the almond meal, sugar, salt, egg, and brandy, if desired, until well blended. Stir in the butter and beat until smooth.

2. TO MAKE THE PASTRY: Preheat the oven to 400°F.

3. Line a baking sheet with parchment paper or leave ungreased. Lightly flour the paper or baking sheet. Place one puff pastry circle in the center and brush some of the beaten egg in a 1-inch border around the edge. Mound the filling in the center of the circle and spread it up to ½ inch from the border. Place the bean in the filling, if desired. Arrange the other round on top, and use a fork to press the edges together. Use the tip of a paring knife to form the outline of a crown (or, after the galette is baked and ready to serve, decorate the cake with a golden paper crown). Brush the rest of the beaten egg on top. Bake in the lower third of the oven until puffed and deep golden brown, 25 to 30 minutes. Dust with powdered sugar and serve slightly warm or at room temperature.

PASTRY
2 sheets purchased frozen
puff pastry, thawed and
cut into two 9-inch rounds

1 **egg,** slightly beaten

1 **dried lima** or **kidney bean**
(optional)

Powdered sugar for dusting

NOTE. Almond meal is available in the baking section of many supermarkets or in specialty markets such as Trader Joe's in the nut section. One brand is Bob's Red Mill. Almond meal is finely ground blanched almonds.

Since the mid-1960s, many people of African descent have observed the traditions and honored the principles of Kwanzaa, which means "first fruit of the harvest." The seven-day celebration begins on December 26 and lasts through January 1. Families gather with friends and neighbors to share favorite foods, traditional music, and beloved stories, while the children enjoy small gifts and treats.

DECEMBER
18 19 20 21 22 23 24
25 26 27 28 29 30 31
JANUARY
1   2   3   4   5   6   7
8   9   10 11 12 13 14

Seven candles—three green for the lands of Africa, one black for the color of its people, and three red for the blood shed in the struggle for freedom—are arranged in a candle holder called a *kinara*. Each night, a single candle is lit to commemorate an ancient African value. The holiday, both festive and spiritual, fosters strength and community while honoring the past.

KWANZAA

DECEMBER 26 TO JANUARY 1

• • • • • • •

Kwanzaa Puzzle Cookies 118

Misbehavin' Girls Peanut Butter Cookie Sandwiches 120

Brown Sugar Benne Cookies and
North African Mint Tea 121

Sweet Pumpkin and Sesame Seed Cookies 122

Apricot Jam and Coconut Squares 123

Cashew Caramel Cracker Bars 125

Crunchy Nut Caramel Bars 126

Wild Rice and Dried Cherry Muffins 127

Soul-Satisfying Biscuits and Gravy 128

Mama's Yummy Sweet Spoonbread Soufflé 130

Southern Comfort Sweet Potato Pecan Pie 131

Banana Wafer Pudding and Pie 133

Church Supper Carrot Cake with Two Frostings 136

Church Supper Carrot Cake with Pineapple and Walnuts 137

Chocolate Peanut Butter Surprise Cupcakes 138

This scrumptious puzzle is no brainteaser, just a great-tasting peanut butter sugar cookie that leads a double life. For those who like a snappy peanut butter crisp and who have a way with a rolling pin, the puzzle cookie, with its 1/8-inch thickness and multiple pieces, is a tasty challenge and a child's delight. (It needs to be that thin in order to hold its shape while baking.)

Those who savor a thicker cookie with a delicate crumb need look no further. You can make several dozen cookies by rolling the dough to an easy 1/4-inch thickness. They're delightful on their own or with an icy glass of milk.

MAKES 2 PUZZLES OR ABOUT 4 DOZEN COOKIES

Kwanzaa Puzzle Cookies

1 1/4 cups **all-purpose flour**

1/2 teaspoon **baking soda**

1/2 teaspoon **salt**

1/4 cup **unsalted butter,** at room temperature

1/2 cup **smooth peanut butter**

1/2 cup **granulated sugar**

1/2 teaspoon **pure vanilla extract**

3 tablespoons **orange juice**

1/4 teaspoon grated **orange zest**

1. Into a medium bowl, sift together the flour, baking soda, and salt, then lightly whisk and set aside.

2. In a stand mixer set on medium speed, beat the butter and peanut butter until blended and creamy, about 45 seconds. On medium speed, add the sugar and beat until light. Beat in the vanilla, orange juice, and zest until blended, scraping down the sides and bottom of the bowl as necessary. Turn off the mixer, add half the flour mixture, and beat on low speed until blended. Add the remaining flour and beat until blended.

3. Using lightly floured hands, gather the dough into a ball. Divide the ball in half and flatten each into a 6- to 8-inch disk. Wrap each disk in plastic wrap and chill for 2 hours or until firm.

4. Preheat the oven to 350°F. Line a baking sheet with parchment paper or leave ungreased and set aside.

continued

Kwanzaa Puzzle Cookies *continued*

5. TO MAKE PUZZLE COOKIES: Remove one disk of dough from the refrigerator and, if needed, soften slightly for easier handling. Roll the dough into a ⅛-inch-thick, 10-by-10-inch square on a lightly floured board, between 2 pieces of parchment paper or heavy-duty plastic wrap, or on a pastry cloth with a cloth-covered rolling pin. Using a paring knife and a ruler, trim the edges. Using Kwanzaa-themed cookie cutters, randomly form several shapes within the square, then use the paring knife to create puzzlelike shapes around them (see photo). Using a palette knife or thin metal spatula, carefully transfer the cookies to the prepared baking sheet, keeping them in the same location as within the puzzle. Place the cookies about ½ inch apart on the baking sheet.

6. Bake in the middle of the oven until the cookies begin to color, 9 to 11 minutes. Let the cookies firm and cool slightly on the baking sheet before transferring them to a rack to cool completely. Arrange the cookies on a flat plate or tray in the completed puzzle form.

7. TO MAKE TRADITIONAL CUTOUT COOKIES: Roll the dough ¼ inch thick. Lightly dip a 3- or 3½-inch cookie cutter in flour, then firmly press it straight down into the dough. Repeat, cutting the cookies close together to avoid rerolling. Place the cookies about ½ inch apart on the baking sheet. Bake in the middle of the oven until the cookies begin to color, about 22 minutes. Let the cookies firm and cool slightly on the baking sheet before transferring to a rack to cool completely.

• • •

VARIATION

If you're a peanut butter lover, be sure to try Misbehavin' Girls Peanut Butter Cookie Sandwiches. Follow the main recipe for the traditional cutout cookies. Roll the dough out ¼ inch thick and use a 3-inch round cookie or biscuit cutter. Bake as directed and cool the cookies to room temperature. Sandwich the flat sides of two cookies together with a generous tablespoon of the **frosting** featured in CHOCOLATE PEANUT BUTTER SURPRISE CUPCAKES (page 138). The result is worth every calorie.

Family and friends will head directly for the cookie jar to get a taste of these crunchy, candylike brown sugar cookies. Made with only a few ingredients, they honor the simple sesame, or benne, seed. During Kwanzaa, when family stories are retold, serve them alongside a freshly brewed pot of minty North African tea.

The sesame plant, which looks a little like the foxglove, is believed to have originated in Africa. The nutritious seeds were introduced to the American South in the 17th and 18th centuries by West African slaves, who added them to many foods.

MAKES ABOUT 2 DOZEN COOKIES AND 6 SERVINGS TEA

Brown Sugar Benne Cookies
and North African Mint Tea

COOKIES

¾ cup **all-purpose flour**

½ teaspoon **salt**

½ teaspoon **baking soda**

½ cup **vegetable shortening**

2 tablespoons **water**

1 cup firmly packed **dark brown sugar**

¾ cup lightly toasted **sesame seeds** (see Note)

continued

1. TO MAKE THE COOKIES: Preheat the oven to 350°F. Line a baking sheet with parchment paper or grease it lightly and set aside.

2. In a small bowl, whisk together the flour, salt, and baking soda until well blended.

3. In a large saucepan over low heat, combine the shortening and water, stirring occasionally until the shortening melts. Remove from the heat and stir in the brown sugar. Stir in the sesame seeds until blended. Stir in the flour mixture. Drop by teaspoonfuls onto the prepared baking sheet. (If the dough begins to thicken, form the cookies with your hands.)

4. Bake until the cookies are set and are no longer shiny, about 12 minutes. Let the cookies firm and cool slightly on the baking sheet before transferring to a rack to cool completely (or slip the parchment paper with the cookies onto the rack to cool).

continued

Brown Sugar Benne Cookies *continued*

TEA

Scant ⅓ cup loose **green** or **oolong tea**

½ cup fresh medium **mint leaves**

⅓ cup **granulated sugar,** or to taste

6 cups **boiling water**

5. TO MAKE THE TEA: In a prewarmed 6-cup teapot, place the green tea, mint leaves, and sugar. Pour in the boiling water and let steep for 4 to 6 minutes.

NOTE: To toast sesame seeds, preheat the oven to 350°F. Spread the seeds on a rimmed baking sheet and bake until lightly browned, about 8 minutes. Since sesame seeds have a high oil content and can quickly become rancid, it's best to buy them in small amounts and use them relatively quickly. Seeds should be kept in an airtight container in a cool, dry place. If refrigerated, they'll last for up to 6 months, and if frozen, up to 1 year.

● ● ●

VARIATION

To make **Sweet Pumpkin and Sesame Seed Cookies,** follow the main recipe, stirring in ½ cup lightly toasted **pumpkin seeds** with the sesame seeds. (Toast the pumpkin seeds as you did the sesame seeds.) Proceed as directed.

Even people who say they don't bake can successfully stir up these delectable bars. Rich and chewy, they make an ideal treat to serve when neighbors stop by for a Kwanzaa visit or to pack into pretty tins and present when you make your holiday calls.

MAKES THIRTY-TWO 1-BY-2-INCH BARS

Apricot Jam and Coconut Squares

1 cup **all-purpose flour**

¼ cup **granulated sugar**

½ cup firmly packed **light brown sugar**

¼ teaspoon **baking soda**

¼ teaspoon **salt**

⅓ cup chopped **pecans**

½ cup **unsalted butter,** at room temperature, cut into small pieces

¾ cup **sweetened flaked coconut,** such as Baker's Angel Flake

¾ cup plus 2 tablespoons **apricot preserves** or **marmalade**

1. Preheat the oven to 350°F. Lightly grease an 8-by-8-inch metal baking pan with cooking spray. To remove the cookies with ease, line the pan, lengthwise and widthwise, with two 8-inch-wide sheets of parchment paper or foil, shiny side up, leaving a few inches of the paper hanging over the edges.

2. In a medium bowl, mix together the flour, granulated sugar, brown sugar, baking soda, salt, and pecans. Using your fingers or a pastry blender, work the butter into the flour mixture until crumbly. Transfer ½ cup of the mixture to a small bowl, stir in the coconut, and set aside to use as the topping. Transfer the remaining mixture to the prepared pan and press evenly across the bottom of the pan. Bake until the crust begins to brown, about 20 minutes.

3. Spread the hot crust with the apricot preserves. Lightly press the reserved topping onto the preserves, return to the oven, and bake until the coconut is well toasted, about 25 minutes.

4. Transfer to a rack to cool and set, about 1½ hours. Use the parchment paper handles to remove and transfer to a cutting board. Cut into thirty-two 1-by-2-inch bars.

With their flaky crust, smooth caramel filling, and deep chocolate glaze speckled with toasted cashews, these scrumptious cookies are rich, habit-forming, and perfect for gift giving. (In Ghana at Christmastime, the cashew tree grows freely, and in courtyards throughout the country, it's often decorated like a Christmas tree.)

The secret to the flaky crust? It's not complicated pie dough, layers of transparent phyllo, or something even more exotic. No, this crust is made from simple supermarket soda crackers. The crackers take on a taste and appearance that would impress the most discerning cookie connoisseur. (The secret is revealed when the baker inverts the cookies to cut them.)

This recipe requires a 10-by-15-inch jelly roll pan.

MAKES 35 TO 40 BARS

Cashew Caramel Cracker Bars

1¼ cups **butter,** melted, divided

35 **Nabisco Premium Saltine crackers**

1 cup firmly packed **dark brown sugar**

1 can (14 ounces) **sweetened condensed milk**

1 package (12 ounces) **semisweet chocolate chips**

1 cup toasted **unsalted cashews,** chopped medium coarse

1. Preheat the oven to 425°F. To make the cookies easy to remove, line a 10-by-15-inch jelly roll pan with a sheet of foil, shiny side up, leaving a few inches hanging over the long edges. Drizzle ¼ cup melted butter onto the foil-lined pan, and brush to cover the bottom. Arrange the crackers, side by side and evenly spaced, so they completely cover the bottom of the pan (don't worry if there are small gaps).

2. In a medium saucepan over medium heat, combine the remaining 1 cup butter and the brown sugar and bring to a boil. Boil for 2 minutes, until the mixture forms a thick syrup (248°F on a candy thermometer). Remove from the heat and slowly whisk in the condensed milk until blended. Pour the mixture over the crackers, making sure all the crackers are covered.

continued

Cashew Caramel Cracker Bars *continued*

3. Bake for 10 minutes. The top will be bubbly and brown. Remove from the oven, scatter the chocolate chips over the topping, and allow them to melt for 5 minutes. Using the back of a spoon or an offset spatula, spread the chocolate over the surface and sprinkle with the nuts. Using your fingers or the back of a spoon, press the nuts into the chocolate. Freeze until the chocolate sets, about 30 minutes.

4. Remove from the freezer and invert the pan onto a clean surface (don't worry if you lose some nuts from the surface; they'll be great for topping an ice cream sundae or for adding to cookie dough). Carefully peel back the foil to reveal the soda-cracker underside of the cookies. Using a sharp knife, cut the cookies along the cracker outlines. This is easier to do when the cookies have begun to thaw slightly. Invert and cut the squares into quarters for bite-size pieces or thirds for finger-size pieces.

● ● ●

VARIATION
For **Crunchy Nut Caramel Bars,** follow the main recipe, substituting your favorite toasted nuts, such as **hazelnuts, almonds, peanuts,** or **walnuts.**

The sixth day of Kwanzaa, December 31, is traditionally the day when friends and family gather together for traditional music, storytelling, and a harvest-inspired meal. For the feast known as *karamu*, these wild rice and dried cherry muffins make a colorful and flavorful surprise when tucked inside a napkin-lined breadbasket.

MAKES 12 MUFFINS

Wild Rice and Dried Cherry Muffins

1 cup **dried cherries**

2 cups **all-purpose flour**

1½ teaspoons **baking powder**

¾ teaspoon **salt**

2½ teaspoons **dried marjoram**

⅓ cup **unsalted butter**, melted and cooled

1 **egg**, at room temperature

1 cup **buttermilk**

⅓ cup **dark honey**, at room temperature

1 cup cooked **wild rice** (about ½ cup dry)

1. Preheat the oven to 375°F. Line 12 standard muffin cups with liners, or lightly grease with cooking spray. In a small bowl, plump the cherries in hot water for 15 minutes, then drain, coarsely chop, and set aside.

2. In a medium bowl, whisk together the flour, baking powder, and salt until well blended. Add the marjoram and whisk until well blended.

3. In another medium bowl, beat together the butter and egg until blended. Add the buttermilk and honey and beat until blended. Add the buttermilk mixture to the flour mixture and beat until just combined and no large streaks of flour remain, scraping down the sides and bottom of the bowl as needed. Fold in the cherries and rice.

4. Divide the batter among the muffin cups. Bake until the muffins rise and become lightly browned, and a toothpick inserted in the middle comes out clean, about 25 minutes. Do not overbake. Cool the muffins in the tin for 5 minutes, then transfer to a rack to cool slightly (otherwise, you could burn your mouth on the hot cherries). These muffins are best served warm on the day you bake them.

Crisp on the outside, soft and flaky on the inside, these hot-from-the-oven buttermilk biscuits make a hungry man smile and the sassiest child quiet with anticipation. Sister Edna likes to fix them after church with her homemade sausage gravy for Sunday noon supper. These satisfying treats are enough to fill up anyone lucky enough to sit at her Sunday table.

MAKES 12 TO 16 BISCUITS AND 3 CUPS GRAVY, SERVING 4 TO 6

Soul-Satisfying Biscuits and Gravy

GRAVY

12 ounces bulk **pork sausage,** plain, spicy, or seasoned as you prefer

¾ cup chopped **onion** (1 small)

¼ cup **all-purpose flour**

2¼ cups **milk**

Salt and freshly ground **black pepper**

1. TO MAKE THE GRAVY: In a heavy saucepan over medium heat, sauté the sausage, breaking it up and turning as needed, until well crumbled and browned. Using a slotted spoon, transfer the cooked sausage to a paper towel to drain. Pour off the drippings, leaving at least 2 tablespoons in the skillet (adding vegetable oil or butter, if needed). Stir in the onion, reduce the heat to medium-low, and cover. Cook, stirring occasionally, until the onions are slightly caramelized, about 20 minutes. Increase the heat to medium-high. Sprinkle the flour over the onions and stir until the flour has blended into the fat and the onions. Cook for 1 minute. Stir in the milk, a little at a time, whisking constantly, until the sauce thickens. Add the sausage, reserving ½ cup for garnishing. Season to taste with salt and pepper, and set aside.

BISCUITS

2 cups **all-purpose flour**

2 teaspoons **baking powder**

¾ teaspoon **baking soda**

½ teaspoon **salt**

¼ cup cold **vegetable shortening,** cut into ¼-inch cubes

¾ cup **buttermilk**

¼ cup **unsalted butter,** melted (optional)

Freshly **chopped parsley** for garnish (optional)

Tabasco sauce for garnish (optional)

2. TO MAKE THE BISCUITS: Preheat the oven to 350°F. Line a baking sheet with parchment paper or leave ungreased and set aside.

3. In a medium bowl, whisk together the flour, baking powder, baking soda, and salt until well blended. Using your fingers or a pastry blender, work the shortening into the flour mixture until it resembles fine crumbs.

4. Make a well in the center of the flour-butter mixture and add the buttermilk all at once, stirring until it forms a soft, sticky ball. Turn out onto a lightly floured work surface. Using lightly floured hands, gently form a ball, then gently knead the dough a couple of times, and pat it out ¾ inch thick. Using a 2-inch biscuit cutter, cut the dough straight down into even rounds. Pat the scraps together and cut out more rounds. If desired, for crisp tops, brush the biscuit tops with melted butter, then place the biscuits, buttered side up, ½ inch apart on the baking sheet. Bake in the upper third of the oven until lightly golden on top, 10 to 12 minutes.

5. TO ASSEMBLE: During the last 5 minutes the biscuits are baking, reheat the gravy over low to medium heat until hot, stirring as needed. Place 3 to 4 hot biscuits on a plate and divide the gravy over them. Garnish with the reserved sausage and parsley, if desired. For added zip, streak the top with Tabasco sauce.

One part cornbread, one part soufflé, this spoonbread has no equal. My friend Jane Zwinger says, "It's cornbread on a cloud." The billowy, crusty soufflé can accompany any meal, from breakfast (drizzled with honey or warm maple syrup) to a light lunch (accompanied with a simple green salad or rich bean soup) to a hearty supper of baked ham and redeye gravy.

SERVES 6

Mama's Yummy Sweet Spoonbread Soufflé

2 cups **whole milk**

3 tablespoons **honey**

Two 4-inch sprigs **sage** with 10 to 12 leaves, lightly crushed in your hand

1 cup **yellow cornmeal**

2 tablespoons **unsalted butter,** at room temperature

¾ teaspoon **salt**

½ teaspoon **baking powder**

4 **eggs,** separated while cold, at room temperature

1. Preheat the oven to 375°F. Butter a 2-quart soufflé dish, including the top edges, and set aside.

2. In a 1½-quart saucepan over medium-high heat, heat the milk, honey, and sage until tiny bubbles form around the edge. Remove from the heat, cover, and steep for 20 to 25 minutes. Remove the sage sprigs and reheat the milk to a simmer over medium heat. Whisk in the cornmeal in a slow, steady stream and continue to whisk until thick, smooth, and lump free, about 2 minutes.

3. Transfer the cornmeal to a mixing bowl, and while still warm, stir in the butter, salt, and baking powder. Cool to lukewarm, then stir in the egg yolks until the mixture is smooth and blended.

4. In another bowl, beat the egg whites until stiff peaks just form. Do not overbeat. Gently stir one-third of the whites into the batter to lighten the batter. Fold in the remaining egg whites until just incorporated and no large white streaks remain. Spoon the batter into the prepared baking dish and bake on the center rack until golden brown and puffed, 35 to 40 minutes. Serve immediately.

Sweet potatoes and pecans are a natural combination, each enhancing the other. This homespun pie is a delicious indulgence after the evening candle lighting or an impressive finale to a come-one, come-all Kwanzaa feast. The contrast of textures is immensely satisfying—the flaky piecrust, the creamy custard laced with bourbon, and the crunchy, pralinelike texture of the sweetened pecans add up to perfection.

SERVES 8

Southern Comfort Sweet Potato Pecan Pie

CANDIED PECANS

1 tablespoon **unsalted butter**

¼ cup plus 2 tablespoons firmly packed **light brown sugar**

1 tablespoon **water**

Small pinch of **cayenne pepper**

1 cup **pecan halves**

continued

1. TO MAKE THE CANDIED PECANS: Preheat the oven to 350°F. Line a baking sheet with foil or parchment paper and set aside.

2. In a small saucepan, melt the butter over medium heat. Stir in the brown sugar, water, and cayenne until blended. Add the nuts and toss to coat. Transfer the nuts to the baking sheet and arrange in a single layer. Bake for 8 minutes. Remove, toss the nuts, and return to the oven so that more of the sugar can bake onto the nuts, about 5 minutes. Slide the foil and nuts off the baking sheet and onto a rack. After the nuts are cool, coarsely chop and set aside.

continued

Sweet Potato Pecan Pie *continued*

CRUST

1 cup **all-purpose flour**

½ teaspoon **salt**

¼ cup cold **vegetable shortening,** cut into small pieces

3 tablespoons cold **unsalted butter,** cut into small pieces

3 to 4 tablespoons **ice water** plus another 1 to 2 teaspoons if needed

FILLING

2 **eggs,** at room temperature

2 cups mashed and lump-free cooked **sweet potatoes** (about 1½ pounds)

¾ cup **granulated sugar**

½ teaspoon **salt**

1 teaspoon **ground ginger**

½ teaspoon **ground allspice**

½ teaspoon **pure vanilla extract**

2 tablespoons **bourbon,** preferably Southern Comfort

½ cup **evaporated milk**

3. TO MAKE THE CRUST: In a medium bowl, whisk together the flour and salt. Add the shortening and butter. Using your fingers or a pastry blender, work the shortening and butter into the flour mixture until crumbly and some pea-size pieces of fat remain. If time permits, chill the flour mixture for 30 minutes.

4. Drizzle the ice water over the flour mixture, 1 tablespoon at a time, mixing until all the flour is moistened and the pastry just clears the side of the bowl (1 to 2 teaspoons water can be added if needed). Using lightly floured hands, gather the dough into a ball. Shape into a disk, wrap in plastic wrap, and chill for 1 hour.

5. Remove the dough from the refrigerator and, if needed, soften slightly for easier handling. Roll the dough out to a 12-inch circle on a lightly floured board, between 2 sheets of parchment paper or heavy-duty plastic wrap, or on a pastry cloth with a cloth-covered rolling pin. Transfer the dough to a 9-inch pie pan and ease into the pan. Trim the overhanging edge of pastry about ¼ inch from the pan's rim. Chill the crust while making the filling.

6. Preheat the oven to 350°F.

7. TO MAKE THE FILLING: In a stand mixer or with a hand mixer set on medium speed, beat the eggs for about 30 seconds. Beat in the sweet potatoes, sugar, salt, ginger, allspice, vanilla, bourbon, and the evaporated milk until smooth and blended.

8. Place the prepared pie shell on a baking sheet. Pour the filling into the chilled pie shell. Bake in the lower third of the oven until the filling is puffed and lightly cracked around the edges and a knife inserted near the center comes out clean, about 1 hour. Transfer to a rack. While the pie is still warm, distribute the nuts over the top and press in lightly to form an even crust. Let cool at least 90 minutes.

As good as an old-fashioned banana wafer pudding is on its own, this recipe rearranges the homey ingredients into a company's-coming holiday pie. Crushing the wafers—and adding a few goodies besides—creates a sweet, crunchy crust just right for holding the smooth-as-silk banana custard pudding, and the high-peaked meringue will have all the guests singing your praises.

MAKES ONE 9-INCH PIE, SERVING 8

Banana Wafer Pudding and Pie

CRUST

About 50 **vanilla wafer cookies,** preferably Nabisco Nilla Wafers

½ cup **sweetened flaked coconut,** such as Baker's Angel Flake (optional)

6 tablespoons **unsalted butter,** melted and cooled

continued

1. TO MAKE THE CRUST: Preheat the oven to 350°F. Lightly grease a 9-inch pie pan with cooking spray and set aside.

2. In the bowl of a food processor, process the cookies until they are fine crumbs. You should have 1½ cups.

3. In a medium bowl, mix together the crumbs, coconut, if desired, and butter until the crumbs are coated. Lightly press the mixture evenly across the bottom of the prepared pie pan. Bake until the crust is golden and crisp, 8 to 10 minutes. Transfer to a rack to cool completely before filling.

continued

Banana Wafer Pudding and Pie *continued*

FILLING

4 **eggs**, at room temperature

1½ teaspoons **pure vanilla extract**

¼ teaspoon **banana extract,** preferably pure

⅔ cup **granulated sugar**

⅓ cup **all-purpose flour**

3 tablespoons **cornstarch**

Pinch of **salt**

2 cups **half-and-half,** divided

MERINGUE

4 **egg whites** (reserved from filling)

⅛ teaspoon **cream of tartar** or distilled vinegar

½ cup **granulated sugar**

2 small, **ripe bananas,** sliced

4. TO MAKE THE FILLING: Separate the eggs, reserving the whites for the meringue. (The whites can remain at room temperature for up to 4 hours.) In a small bowl, whisk together the yolks, vanilla, and banana extract until blended, and set aside.

5. In the top of a double boiler, whisk together the sugar, flour, cornstarch, and salt. Whisk in ¼ cup half-and-half to form a smooth paste. Place over simmering water, and gradually stir in the remaining 1¾ cups half-and-half. Cook, stirring constantly, until the mixture begins to thicken, 7 to 10 minutes. Remove from the heat.

6. Slowly whisk ¼ cup of the hot half-and-half mixture into the egg yolk mixture until blended. Slowly whisk in another ½ cup. Then slowly whisk the hot egg yolk mixture into the remaining hot half-and-half in the top of the double boiler. Place the double boiler over the simmering water and cook until the mixture is quite thick, stirring constantly, about 10 minutes (or until an instant thermometer reads 180°F). Remove from the heat and push through a fine sieve into a bowl. Press plastic wrap onto the filling and chill for 2 hours or longer.

7. TO MAKE THE MERINGUE: In a stand mixer or with a hand mixer set on medium-low speed, beat the 4 reserved room temperature egg whites and cream of tartar until foamy. Increase to high speed and beat in the sugar, 1 tablespoon at a time, until stiff and glossy. Do not overbeat.

8. TO ASSEMBLE: Preheat the oven to 350°F. Spread half the chilled filling in the prepared piecrust. Arrange the sliced bananas to cover the filling. Carefully spread the remaining filling over the bananas. Spread the meringue over the filling, sealing the meringue right up to the edge of the pie plate. Use the back of a spoon to swirl or pull the meringue up into points. Bake until the meringue peaks are a delicate brown, 12 to 15 minutes. Cool away from a draft. Serve immediately. This pie is best when the bananas and meringue are fresh (when the bananas sit in filling too long their water loosens the filling). Refrigerate any remaining pie, and enjoy it within a day.

CAKE

2 cups **all-purpose flour**

1 teaspoon **baking soda**

2 teaspoons **baking powder**

1 teaspoon **salt**

1 tablespoon **unsweetened cocoa powder**

2 teaspoons **ground cinnamon**

½ teaspoon **ground mace**

Once a month, Sunday church led to Sunday school, then choir practice, and finally to our Sunday church supper. Fellowship Hall became one giant dining room, as high schoolers filled the gymnasium with folding tables and chairs, and the ladies' Bible group set about arranging a giant potluck. Ruby Mae Wilson's carrot cake always took the place of honor the dessert table, between Yvonne Smith's sugar pie and Mavis Rivers's devil's food cake. Whenever Ruby made this cake with her Church Lady's Frosting, it was gone before you could say "Amen!"

When you make this cake, choose from either the classic cream cheese frosting or Ruby's coconut and brandy-spiked cream cheese frosting.

MAKES ONE 13-BY-9-INCH CAKE, SERVING 16 TO 24

Church Supper Carrot Cake
with Two Frostings

4 **eggs,** at room temperature

1 cup **vegetable oil**

1 cup firmly packed **dark brown sugar**

1 cup **granulated sugar**

2 teaspoons **pure vanilla extract**

3 cups grated **carrots** (about 3 medium carrots)

¾ teaspoon grated **orange zest**

1 cup **unsweetened grated coconut** (optional)

1 cup **golden raisins,** coarsely chopped (optional)

1. TO MAKE THE CAKE: Preheat the oven to 350°F. Grease and dust with flour a 13-by-9-inch metal cake pan and set aside.

2. Into a medium bowl, sift together the flour, baking soda, baking powder, salt, cocoa, cinnamon, and mace, then lightly whisk and set aside.

3. In a stand mixer set on medium speed, combine the eggs, oil, brown sugar, granulated sugar, and vanilla until blended. Turn off the mixer, add half the flour mixture, and beat on low speed until the mixture is blended. Add the remaining flour and beat until blended, scraping down the sides and bottom of the bowl as necessary. Remove the bowl and stir in the carrots and the orange zest, and the coconut and raisins, if desired. Pour the batter into the prepared pan. Bake until a toothpick inserted in the center comes out clean and the cake begins to pull away from the sides, about 35 minutes. Transfer to a rack to cool completely before frosting. Frost with either CREAM CHEESE FROSTING or CHURCH LADY'S FROSTING.

CREAM CHEESE FROSTING

6 ounces **cream cheese,** at room temperature

¼ cup **unsalted butter,** at room temperature

Pinch of **salt**

1 tablespoon **pure vanilla extract**

¾ teaspoon grated **orange zest** (optional)

4 cups (1 pound) sifted **powdered sugar**

2 teaspoons or more **milk,** if needed

CHURCH LADY'S FROSTING

6 ounces **cream cheese,** at room temperature

½ cup plus 2 tablespoons **unsalted butter,** at room temperature

Pinch of **salt**

2 tablespoons **brandy**

2 teaspoons **pure vanilla extract**

4 cups (1 pound) sifted **powdered sugar**

2 teaspoons or more **milk,** if needed

¾ cup **sweetened flaked coconut,** such as Baker's Angel Flake

4. TO MAKE THE CREAM CHEESE FROSTING: In a stand mixer or with a hand mixer set on medium-low speed, beat the cream cheese, butter, and salt until just combined. Beat in the vanilla, orange zest (if desired), and powdered sugar and continue to beat until it reaches a spreading consistency. If necessary, add more milk for a creamier consistency. The frosting can be used immediately or stored, covered, in the refrigerator for up to 3 days.

TO MAKE THE CHURCH LADY'S FROSTING: In a stand mixer or with a hand mixer set on medium-low speed, beat the cream cheese, butter, and salt until just combined. Beat in the brandy, vanilla, and powdered sugar and continue to beat until it reaches a spreading consistency. If necessary, add a teaspoon or more of milk for a creamier consistency. Stir in the coconut until blended. The frosting can be used immediately or stored, covered, in the refrigerator for up to 3 days.

• • •

VARIATION

If you prefer **Church Supper Carrot Cake** with **Walnuts,** follow the main recipe, adding 1 cup well-drained **crushed pineapple** and 1 cup coarsely chopped **walnuts** to the cake batter.

These five-bite desserts are a frosting lover's paradise. They combine the two most important food groups—chocolate and peanut butter—and both are in good supply. Thanks go to Oregon pastry whiz Marilyn DeVault for sharing the recipe. You'll be glad you made a batch of these cupcakes (and oh yes, there's a wonderful surprise in the middle).

MAKES 12 CUPCAKES

Chocolate Peanut Butter Surprise Cupcakes

CUPCAKES

3 ounces **cream cheese,**
at room temperature

¼ cup **chunky peanut butter**

2 tablespoons **honey**

2 tablespoons **powdered sugar**

1 tablespoon **heavy (whipping) cream**

1 cup **all-purpose flour**

⅓ cup **unsweetened Dutch process cocoa powder**

1 teaspoon **baking soda**

½ teaspoon **salt**

½ cup **unsalted butter,**
at room temperature

1 cup firmly packed
light brown sugar

2 **eggs,** at room temperature

1 teaspoon **pure vanilla extract**

½ cup **buttermilk**

1. **TO MAKE THE CUPCAKES:** Preheat the oven to 350°F. Line 12 standard muffin cups with liners and set aside.

2. In a medium bowl, with a hand mixer or by hand, beat together the cream cheese, peanut butter, honey, powdered sugar, and cream until smooth, and set aside.

3. Into a medium bowl, sift together the flour, cocoa, baking soda, and salt, then lightly whisk and set aside.

4. In a stand mixer set on medium-low speed, beat the butter until creamy, about 30 seconds. On medium speed, beat in the brown sugar until light and lump free. Add the eggs, one at a time, and beat until fully incorporated, scraping down the sides and bottom of the bowl as necessary. Beat in the vanilla until blended. Add the flour mixture in two portions, alternating with the buttermilk in one addition until smooth and just blended.

5. Fill each muffin cup one-third full of batter. Drop a heaping teaspoon of the peanut butter mixture into the center of each cupcake, gently nudging it into the batter. Continue to fill each cup with more batter until each is nearly full.

6. Bake in the center of the oven until the tops spring back when lightly pressed with a fingertip, about 20 minutes. Do not overbake. Cool the cupcakes in the tin for 5 minutes, then transfer to a rack to cool completely before frosting.

FROSTING

2½ tablespoons **unsalted butter,** at room temperature

3 ounces **cream cheese,** at room temperature

¼ cup plus 2 tablespoons **chunky peanut butter**

1¼ teaspoons **pure vanilla extract**

2 cups **powdered sugar**

3 to 4 tablespoons **heavy (whipping) cream**

7. TO MAKE THE FROSTING: In a stand mixer or with a hand mixer set on medium-low speed, beat together the butter, cream cheese, peanut butter, and vanilla until light and fluffy. On the lowest speed, add the powdered sugar alternately with the cream and beat until smooth. Liberally spread the frosting on each cupcake. These cupcakes can be stored at room temperature for 2 to 3 days.

It's New Year's Eve: 10, 9, 8, then 7, 6, 5, 4. The seconds tick by: 3, 2, 1—Happy New Year!

Like a clean slate, New Year's Day offers unlimited possibilities. No wonder people all over the world gather the night before to celebrate. For a few hours, everyday life is put aside, and opportunity reigns supreme.

DECEMBER
25 26 27 28 29 30 **31**
JANUARY
1   2   3   4   5   6   7
8   9   10 11 12 13 14
15 16 17 18 19 20 21

Whether you go to town to whoop it up or stay inside curled by the fire, the last holiday of the old year and the first morning light of the new are times to reflect on the past and anticipate the prospects ahead.

NEW YEAR'S

DECEMBER 31 AND JANUARY 1

• • • • • • •

Petite French Almond Cakes with Champagne 143

Midnight Cowboy Chocolate Chip Cookies 145

Next Year's Fortune Cookies 146

Slivered Biscotti with Gelato Affogato 148

Walnut Walkaways 149
Currant, Orange, and Pine Nut Walkaways 150
Grapefruit, Tangerine, and Slivered Almond Walkaways 150
Candied Ginger, Lemon Zest, and Walnut Walkaways 150

Triple-Treat Touchdown Bars 151
Triple-Treat Almond Bars 152

Dutch Baby Pancake 153
Spiced Blueberry Sauce 154
Strawberry Orange Morning Relish 154

Bloody Mary and Baked Mushroom Omelet 155

New Year's Eve Meringue Roulade 157

Start-the-New-Year-with-Chocolate Brownie Terrine 161

The candles are lit, the champagne is chilled. Now capture the romance of New Year's Eve with a French connection. These golden sweets look like a cookie, taste like a cake, and are delicately reminiscent of another French beauty, the madeleine.

The recipe comes from Dominique Geulin, one of my favorite Oregon bakers. Every morning at his St. Honoré Boulangerie in northwest Portland, he makes these popular French almond cakes, known as *friands aux amandes*. Though they're traditionally baked in canoe-shaped molds, Dominique adapted the recipe for us by using a mini muffin tin. *Merci, Dominique.*

MAKES ABOUT 30 BITE-SIZE CAKES

Petite French Almond Cakes with Champagne

1 cup **almond meal** (see Note)

½ cup plus 2 tablespoons **all-purpose flour**

¾ cup **egg whites** (from 5 to 6 eggs), at room temperature

1 cup **granulated sugar**

1 tablespoon **honey**, at room temperature (see Note)

⅓ cup plus 1 teaspoon **unsalted butter**, melted and cooled

Powdered sugar for dusting (optional)

Champagne for toasting

1. In a small bowl, whisk together the almond meal and flour until well blended, and set aside.

2. In a stand mixer on medium speed, whisk the egg whites. When the whites change from a loose to a slightly loose foam, slowly add the sugar in a steady sprinkle, over 4 to 6 minutes. This takes practice; do not overbeat. You want the whites to be glossy and moist. (When the whisk attachment is lifted, it will hold a peak.)

3. Sift the flour mixture over the egg whites in 3 or 4 portions, folding each addition in gently before adding the next. Use long, light strokes. Fold in the honey, followed by the cool melted butter. The batter should be glossy, light, and smooth. Cover with plastic wrap, and allow the batter to rest at room temperature for 30 minutes.

continued

Petite French Almond Cakes *continued*

4. Preheat the oven to 400°F. Thoroughly brush the cups of a mini muffin tin with additional melted butter, sift all-purpose flour over the molds to cover them, then invert over the sink and tap several times to shake out the excess. (Or, if you prefer, line the cups with cupcake papers.) Gently spoon the batter into the molds (or use a pastry bag), filling them three-quarters full.

5. Bake in the center of the oven until golden brown, 8 to 10 minutes. Transfer to a rack to cool for 5 minutes. The sides will begin to pull away from the pan. Remove the cakes from the tin to cool completely. Sprinkle with powdered sugar, if desired, and serve with champagne. The cakes are best the day they are baked, but they can be stored in an airtight container for 2 to 3 days.

NOTE: Almond meal is available in the baking section of many supermarkets or in specialty markets such as Trader Joe's in the nut section. One brand is Bob's Red Mill. Almond meal is finely ground blanched almonds.

The honey needs to be at room temperature or slightly warmer, so that it easily runs out of the measuring spoon.

Okay, all you cowboys. You've trotted through most of this book, pretending it didn't matter that there wasn't a chocolate chip cookie recipe in the roundup. Now's the time to get out the mixing bowl and rustle up those chocolate chips. Whether you're home on the range with the posse or in the ranch house with your favorite partner, these lil' doggies will hit the spot as you hit the New Year's trail.

MAKES 3 TO 4 DOZEN COOKIES

Midnight Cowboy Chocolate Chip Cookies

1 cup **all-purpose flour**

1 teaspoon **baking soda**

1 teaspoon **baking powder**

½ teaspoon **salt**

1 cup **smooth peanut butter**

1 cup **vegetable shortening**

1 cup **granulated sugar**

¾ cup firmly packed **light brown sugar**

2 teaspoons **pure vanilla extract**

2 **eggs,** at room temperature

1 cup old-fashioned rolled **oats**

2 cups (12 ounces) **semisweet chocolate chips**

1 cup chopped **pecans**

1 cup **sweetened flaked coconut**

1. Preheat the oven to 350°F. Line a baking sheet with parchment paper or leave ungreased and set aside.

2. Into a medium bowl, whisk together the flour, baking soda, baking powder, and salt and set aside.

3. In a stand mixer or with a hand mixer set on low speed, beat the peanut butter and shortening until creamy. On medium speed, add the granulated and brown sugars and beat until light and lump free. Beat in the vanilla and then the eggs, one at a time, until fully blended, scraping down the sides and bottom of the bowl as necessary. Turn off the mixer, add half the flour mixture, and beat on low speed until blended. Add the remaining flour and beat until blended. Stir in the oats, chocolate chips, pecans, and coconut.

4. Drop by large tablespoonfuls onto the prepared baking sheet, leaving 2½ inches between the mounds of dough. Bake until golden brown, 15 to 17 minutes. Cool for several minutes on the baking sheet before transferring to a rack, or carefully pull the parchment paper from the pan and place it, along with the cookies, on the rack.

"Good fortune comes to those who write the fortunes," read the tiny slip of paper.

At year's end, the time is ripe for making fortune cookies. Here's your chance to predict the future, reveal a secret, or hint at something really juicy.

Just for the fun of it, instead of the traditional fortune cookie shape, these delicate, orange-scented cookies are rolled, cigarette-style. So, after you've written your prophetic message, just roll it up and tuck it into the cookie's hollow center. For best results, use a reusable nonstick baking sheet liner, such as a Silpat. It completely prevents these cookies from sticking.

MAKES 12 TO 16 COOKIES

Next Year's Fortune Cookies

½ cup **all-purpose** flour

1 tablespoon **cornstarch**

¼ cup **granulated sugar**

Pinch of **salt**

¼ cup **vegetable oil**

2 **egg whites,** at room temperature

1 tablespoon plus 1 teaspoon **Grand Marnier** or other orange-flavored liqueur

1 teaspoon **pure vanilla extract**

½ teaspoon grated **orange zest** (about ½ medium orange)

1. Preheat the oven to 325°F. Line a baking sheet with a reusable nonstick sheet liner or parchment paper and set aside.

2. In a medium bowl, whisk together the flour, cornstarch, sugar, and salt until well blended. Add the oil, egg whites, liqueur, vanilla, and orange zest. Beat at high speed until smooth.

3. Start with just 2 cookies at a time, dropping the batter by level tablespoons about 3 inches apart on the baking sheet. Using the back of a spoon, spread each portion into a 4-inch-diameter cookie. Bake until the edges start to brown, 8 to 10 minutes.

4. Using a wide, thin, flexible spatula, lift each cookie off the baking sheet. (If it begins to bunch or tear, let it cool for another 15 to 20 seconds. Or if it cools too much on the pan, return the pan to the oven to resoften for about 1 minute.) Using your fingers, roll the hot cookie into a cylinder. Have a bowl of ice water close by to keep your fingertips cool. Place seamside down on a rack to cool completely. Repeat with the remaining batter. Before serving, slip a fortune into the hollow center of each cookie.

As the winter holidays wind to a festive close, you may be ready to ditch those over-the-top desserts. I, for one, like to ring out the old year with a simpler celebration, and this combination is irresistible. The enjoyably brittle biscotti are adult cookies worthy of kidlike dunking, and the *gelato affogato* is the perfect plunge. So go ahead, dip your biscotti down, and revel in the cool, hot, and creamy layers.

MAKES ABOUT 22 BISCOTTI AND 2 SERVINGS GELATO AFFOGATO

Slivered Biscotti with Gelato Affogato

BISCOTTI

1½ cups **all-purpose flour**

⅔ cup **almond meal** (see Note)

¾ cup **granulated sugar**

1 teaspoon **ground cardamom**

1 teaspoon **baking powder**

¼ teaspoon **salt**

2 **eggs,** at room temperature

1 teaspoon **pure almond extract**

2 to 2½ teaspoons **water,** if necessary

GELATO AFFOGATO

2 small scoops **vanilla-bean ice cream**

2 to 4 shots hot **espresso**

⅓ cup lightly sweetened softly **whipped cream** (optional)

1. TO MAKE THE BISCOTTI: Preheat the oven to 350°F. Line a baking sheet with parchment paper or grease it lightly and set aside.

2. In a large bowl, whisk together the flour, almond meal, sugar, cardamom, baking powder, and salt. In a small bowl, whisk together the eggs and almond extract until well blended. Add the egg mixture to the flour mixture and stir until the dough is crumbly, adding a few drops of water if necessary. Using lightly floured hands, gather the dough into a rough ball.

3. Divide the dough in half. Form each portion into a tightly packed log about 8 inches long. Transfer the logs to the baking sheet, about 4 inches apart, and slightly flatten each to make about a 2½-inch loaf. Bake until just firm when pressed in the center, about 25 minutes. Transfer to a rack to cool for 10 minutes. Lower the oven temperature to 325°F.

4. Carefully transfer the loaves to a cutting board. Using a serrated knife, cut each loaf diagonally into ½-inch slices. Lay the slices flat on the baking sheet and return them to the oven. Bake for 15 minutes. Transfer to a rack to cool completely.

5. TO MAKE THE GELATO AFFOGATO: In 2 clear, sturdy drinking or juice glasses, add 1 scoop of ice cream. Pour the hot espresso over the ice cream, and top with the whipped cream, if desired.

NOTE: Almond meal, or finely ground almonds, is available in many supermarkets, such as Trader Joe's. One brand is Bob's Red Mill.

Is it a cookie? Is it a Danish? These are questions to contemplate, bite after bite.

"I serve them whenever I want to impress someone—and they're not even that difficult to make," says my friend David Kobos. The cookie dough is lightly flavored with yeast that is proofed but not allowed to rise. It's an intriguing and delicious addition. Hmm, pass me another.

MAKES ABOUT 2 DOZEN COOKIES

Walnut Walkaways

DOUGH

2 to 2¼ teaspoons (1 package) **active dry yeast**

1 teaspoon **granulated sugar**

¼ cup **warm water** (110°F)

2 cups **all-purpose flour**

⅛ teaspoon **salt**

¾ cup cold **unsalted butter**

1 large **egg**, lightly beaten

FILLING

5 ounces **cream cheese,** at room temperature

½ cup **granulated sugar**

Grated zest of 1 small **orange**

Grated zest of 1 medium **lemon**

½ cup plus 2 tablespoons finely **chopped walnuts,** divided

Powdered sugar for dusting

1. TO MAKE THE DOUGH: In a small bowl, mix together the yeast, sugar, and warm water, and let stand until foamy, 5 to 10 minutes.

2. In a food processor, pulse together the flour and salt a few times to mix. Cut the butter into tablespoon-size chunks, add to the flour mixture, and pulse until the mixture resembles coarse crumbs. Add the yeast mixture and the egg, and process just until the dough forms a ball. Do not overprocess. (If working by hand, combine the flour and salt in a bowl and cut in the butter until the mixture resembles coarse crumbs. Stir in the yeast mixture and egg until the dough comes together.) Transfer the dough to a large, lightly greased bowl and turn the dough to grease the top. Cover the bowl with plastic wrap and chill for 1 hour.

3. TO MAKE THE FILLING: In a small bowl, beat together the cream cheese, sugar, orange zest, and lemon zest until light and fluffy.

continued

4. TO ASSEMBLE: Preheat the oven to 375°F. Line a baking sheet with parchment paper or grease it lightly and set aside.

5. Remove the dough from the refrigerator. Divide the dough in half. Roll each portion into a 9-by-13-inch rectangle on a lightly floured board, between 2 sheets of parchment paper or heavy-duty plastic wrap, or on a pastry cloth with a cloth-covered rolling pin. Spread half the cream cheese mixture on each rectangle, then sprinkle each with ¼ cup walnuts.

6. Roll up each rectangle, starting with a long side, jelly roll fashion, and pinch the edges together to seal. Place seam side down on the prepared baking sheet. Using a sharp knife, make a lengthwise slit halfway through each roll. Sprinkle the exposed opening with the remaining 2 tablespoons nuts. Bake until lightly golden, about 25 minutes. Cool on the baking sheet. Dust with powdered sugar and slice each roll on the diagonal into 1-inch-wide pieces.

• • •

VARIATIONS

For Currant, Orange, and Pine Nut Walkaways, follow the main recipe. For the filling, mix together 5 ounces **cream cheese,** 1 teaspoon grated **orange zest,** ½ teaspoon **ground cinnamon,** 4 teaspoons **dried currants,** and ½ cup finely chopped **pine nuts.** Continue as directed.

For Grapefruit, Tangerine, and Slivered Almond Walkaways, follow the main recipe. For the filling, mix together 5 ounces **cream cheese,** 1 teaspoon grated **grapefruit zest,** 2 teaspoons grated **tangerine zest,** and ½ cup finely chopped **slivered almonds.** Continue as directed.

For Candied Ginger, Lemon Zest, and Walnut Walkaways, follow the main recipe. For the filling, mix together 5 ounces **cream cheese,** 4 teaspoons chopped **candied ginger,** 1 teaspoon grated **lemon zest,** and ½ cup finely chopped **walnuts.** Continue as directed.

Diet? What's that? Be in the moment, and don't sweat the calories. Your favorite Bowl team is close to that tie-breaking touchdown, so grab the last rich square of brownielike badness. (Think of it as a "Hail Mary" play on the field, and your prayers will be answered.)

These oldie-but-goodie chocolate bars are high-scoring in my book as well as in my friend Arlene Schnitzer's. "A meal without chocolate is a meal I don't want," Arlene sagely pronounced when she first served them at a dinner party more than a decade ago.

MAKES 30 SMALL SQUARES

Triple-Treat Touchdown Bars

CAKE

2 ounces **unsweetened chocolate**

½ cup **unsalted butter**

½ cup **all-purpose flour**

¼ teaspoon **salt**

2 **eggs,** at room temperature

1 cup **granulated sugar**

¼ teaspoon **pure peppermint extract**

continued

1. Preheat the oven to 350°F. Lightly grease an 8-by-8-inch baking pan with cooking spray. To help remove the cookies, line the pan, lengthwise and widthwise, with two 8-inch-wide sheets of parchment paper or foil, shiny side up, leaving a few inches of the paper hanging over the edges. Lightly grease with cooking spray.

2. TO MAKE THE CAKE: In the top of a double boiler, melt the chocolate and butter and set aside to cool slightly. In a small bowl, whisk together the flour and salt until blended.

3. In a medium bowl, whisk the eggs and sugar until well blended. Stir in the melted chocolate mixture and the peppermint extract. Stir in the flour mixture until blended. Pour the batter into the prepared baking pan. Bake in the center of the oven until firm to the touch and a toothpick inserted in the middle comes out just clean, about 20 minutes. Transfer to a rack to cool.

continued

Triple-Treat Touchdown Bars *continued*

FROSTING

2 tablespoons **unsalted butter, at room temperature**

1 cup **powdered sugar**

1 tablespoon **heavy (whipping) cream** or **half-and-half**

½ teaspoon **pure peppermint extract**

TOPPING

2 ounces **unsweetened chocolate**

1 tablespoon **unsalted butter**

4. TO MAKE THE FROSTING: In a medium bowl, beat together the butter, powdered sugar, cream, and peppermint extract until it reaches a spreading consistency. Spread over the top of the cooled cake. Chill for 30 minutes.

5. TO MAKE THE TOPPING: In the microwave or in a saucepan over low heat, melt the chocolate and the butter, stirring to combine. Drizzle the mixture over the frosting, then tilt the pan so the topping covers the frosting. Chill until the chocolate is firm, then cut into small squares.

• • •

VARIATION

For Triple-Treat Almond Bars, follow the main recipe, substituting ½ teaspoon **pure vanilla extract** for the ¼ teaspoon peppermint extract in the cake. In the frosting, substitute **almond extract** for the peppermint, and sprinkle the topping with **toasted sliced almonds.**

I don't want to think too hard on New Year's Day morning. I just want to start the year off right, with something fabulous to eat and effortless to make, a dish to woo and to chew that sets this day apart. A Dutch baby pancake springs to mind. Baked in an ovenproof skillet, the thin, eggy batter puffs up like a popover, making a grand greeting to the all-new year.

While most people prefer a simple dusting of powdered sugar followed by a squeeze of fresh lemon juice, I've also included two special toppings. For best results, it's important to have all the ingredients at room temperature. (I've been known to shorten this step by submerging the eggs in a small bowl of warm water for 5 minutes and microwaving the milk for about 30 seconds.)

SERVES 2 TO 4

Dutch Baby Pancake

3 **eggs,** at room temperature

¾ cup **milk,** at room temperature

¾ cup **all-purpose flour**

¼ teaspoon **salt**

2½ tablespoons **unsalted butter**

Powdered sugar for dusting

Lemon wedges for serving
(optional)

SPICED BLUEBERRY SAUCE and/or
STRAWBERRY ORANGE MORNING
RELISH for serving (optional;
page 154)

1. Preheat the oven to 400°F for 20 to 30 minutes.

2. In a small bowl, lightly whisk the eggs until they change color. Whisk in the milk. In a medium bowl, whisk together the flour and salt until well blended. Gently whisk the egg mixture into the flour mixture until only small lumps remain, and set aside.

3. Place the butter in the bottom of a heavy, 12-inch ovenproof skillet. Place the skillet in the center of the oven until the butter is melted and the pan is hot.

4. Using an oven mitt, remove the skillet. Holding the skillet's handle, tilt the skillet so the butter swirls and coats the bottom and lower sides. Lightly whisk the batter, then pour it into the skillet and return the skillet to the oven. Bake until puffed and golden brown, about 20 minutes. Avoid opening the oven door, if possible, although you can sneak a peek if you must. Dust with powdered sugar and serve immediately, cutting the pancake into wedges. At the table, accompany with lemon wedges, SPICED BLUEBERRY SAUCE, and/or STRAWBERRY ORANGE MORNING RELISH.

SPICED BLUEBERRY SAUCE

I like this sauce over pancakes and waffles, but it's also delicious as an ice-cream topping or as an accent to savory entrées such as pork tenderloin.

MAKES ABOUT 2 CUPS

4 cups frozen or fresh **blueberries**

2 teaspoons **ground ginger**

1 teaspoon **ground cinnamon**

1/4 cup **granulated sugar**

1 tablespoon **water**

1 tablespoon freshly squeezed **lemon juice**

In a medium, heavy saucepan, combine the blueberries, ginger, cinnamon, sugar, water, and lemon juice. Bring the mixture to a boil over medium heat, stirring occasionally. Let it boil slowly until thickened, about 5 minutes. Remove from the heat and serve warm.

STRAWBERRY ORANGE MORNING RELISH

Every once in awhile, in the middle of winter, our neighborhood supermarket has imported fresh strawberries. When it does, and I feel like splurging, this sweet relish is a welcome surprise alongside a Dutch baby or French toast.

MAKES ABOUT 1½ CUPS

3 to 4 large **navel oranges**

2 tablespoons **Grand Marnier** or other orange-flavored liqueur

2 cups **fresh strawberries,** hulled and sliced

2 tablespoons **granulated sugar**

½ cup **currant jelly**

¼ teaspoon freshly squeezed **lemon juice,** or to taste

1. Peel the oranges and cut crosswise into 5 or 6 slices. Layer the slices in a shallow serving bowl, drizzle with the liqueur, and set aside. In a small bowl, combine the strawberries and sugar, and set aside for 30 minutes.

2. In a small saucepan over medium-low heat, melt the jelly, and stir in the lemon juice. Pour the warm jelly over the strawberries and mix well. Spoon the strawberries and sauce over the oranges and set aside for at least 45 minutes, or chill for 1 to 2 hours before serving.

This baked omelet can work its satisfying magic in many ways—as a get-the-juices-flowing breakfast, a hair-of-the-dog hors d'oeuvre, or a minutes-to-midnight late night meal. The crowning glory is a warm, boozy salsa that's spooned over each savory, mushroomy wedge. Be sure to make the sauce several hours ahead, or the day before, so the flavors have a chance to mellow and blend. Then, just before serving, toss in another jigger for a bloody great taste.

SERVES 8

Bloody Mary and Baked Mushroom Omelet

BLOODY MARY SAUCE

2 tablespoons **extra-virgin olive oil**

1 cup diced **yellow onion**

Pinch of **red pepper flakes**

2 cloves **garlic,** minced

1 can (28 ounces) diced **tomatoes,** with their juices

¼ cup plus 2 tablespoons **vodka,** divided

3 tablespoons **tomato paste**

½ cup **water,** or more if needed

2 sprigs **thyme**

3 big sprigs **celery leaves**

4 sprigs **parsley**

continued

1. TO MAKE THE BLOODY MARY SAUCE: In a saucepan over medium heat, heat the olive oil and sauté the onions and red pepper flakes until the onions are golden, about 5 minutes. Stir in the garlic and sauté for 30 seconds. Stir in the tomatoes with their juices, ¼ cup vodka, tomato paste, and water. Using kitchen string, tie the thyme, celery leaf, and parsley sprigs together to form a bouquet garni, and add it to the tomato mixture. Slowly simmer, uncovered, for 30 minutes, stirring occasionally and adding more water if necessary. The sauce should be thick. Remove the bouquet garni and discard. Cool, cover, and refrigerate for several hours or overnight. To serve, reheat and stir in the remaining 2 tablespoons vodka. Makes about 3 cups.

continued

Bloody Mary and Baked Mushroom Omelet *continued*

OMELET

2 tablespoons **unsalted butter**

¾ cup diced **yellow onion**

1 pound **white mushrooms,** sliced (about 5 cups)

1½ teaspoons **dried thyme**

¾ cup **heavy (whipping) cream** or **half-and-half**

Salt and freshly ground **black pepper**

8 **eggs,** at room temperature

1½ cups grated **fontina cheese** (about 6 ounces)

2. TO MAKE THE OMELET: Preheat the oven to 425°F. Lightly butter a 10-inch springform pan, place it on a jelly roll–style baking sheet, and set aside. (To avoid leaks, make sure the springform latch is secure and properly closed.)

3. In a large skillet over medium-high heat, melt the butter. When it is hot, add the onions and sauté until just golden, about 5 minutes. Stir in the mushrooms and thyme and continue to sauté until the mushrooms are browned and no liquid remains. Stir in the cream. Taste and adjust the seasoning with salt and pepper.

4. In a large bowl, vigorously whisk the eggs. Gently whisk in the mushroom mixture until well blended, then stir in the cheese. Pour into the prepared springform pan. Bake in the center of the oven until the top is golden and firm, 30 to 35 minutes.

5. Remove and transfer the springform pan to a rack to cool for 10 minutes. Using a paring knife, loosen the omelet from the inside edge of the pan. To serve, gently unlatch the sides of the springform pan and serve the omelet on the pan base. Serve warm or at room temperature, cut into thin wedges and accompanied by the BLOODY MARY SAUCE.

A stunning dessert, this white-upon-white meringue roulade is understated simplicity at its best. The creamy mascarpone filling is delicately accented with orange flower water, which gives it a beguilingly ethereal taste. If you prefer a flourish or a flounce, choose one of the fresh fruit medleys. A satiny ribbon of dark chocolate sauce also makes an elegant statement.

SERVES 8

New Year's Eve Meringue Roulade

MERINGUE

8 **egg whites,** at room temperature

½ teaspoon **cream of tartar**

1¾ cup **baker's** or **superfine sugar** (see Note)

2 teaspoons **cornstarch**

2 teaspoons **pure vanilla extract**

Powdered sugar for dusting

continued

1. TO MAKE THE MERINGUE: Preheat the oven to 350°F. Line the bottom and sides of a 10-by-15-inch jelly roll pan with parchment paper and grease it lightly. Lightly grease the top rim of the pan and set aside.

2. In a stand mixer set on medium-low speed, beat the egg whites and cream of tartar until foamy. Increase to high speed, slowly add the sugar, and beat until glossy, stiff peaks form. Dust the meringue with the cornstarch, then fold it in with the vanilla.

3. Smooth the meringue into the prepared pan and bake for 30 minutes. It will be puffy and high. Cool for 5 minutes, then loosen any edges that stick to the pan. Gently turn it over onto a sheet of parchment dusted with powdered sugar. Cool for 10 minutes, then peel off the paper.

continued

FILLING

8 ounces **mascarpone**

¼ cup **heavy (whipping) cream**

3 tablespoons **baker's** or **superfine sugar** (see Note)

1 to 2 teaspoons **orange flower water** (see Note)

SUGGESTED FRUIT TOPPING MEDLEYS

Raspberries, blackberries, and **blueberries**

Kiwi, green grapes, and **strawberries**

Blackberries, passionfruit pulp, and **mint**

4. TO MAKE THE FILLING: In a medium bowl, mix together the mascarpone, cream, and sugar until blended. Stir in 1 teaspoon orange flower water until blended. Taste, adding additional orange flower water in drops as needed.

5. TO ASSEMBLE: Spread the filling over the meringue. Beginning at a short side, carefully roll up the meringue, using the parchment paper to support it. Chill for 2 to 3 hours before serving. Slice the roulade, and serve it plain or with any of the suggested fruit toppings. It is best served within 4 hours.

NOTES: Baker's or superfine sugar is available in supermarket baking sections. For a quick substitute, whirl 1 cup of granulated sugar at a time in a processor or blender until fine, about 20 seconds.

Orange flower water is available in supermarket liquor sections. It is an aromatic distillation of bitter-orange blossoms and is used as a flavoring.

If ever there were a gorgeously wicked finale to the old year, it would have to be Jeremy Karp's chocolate brownie terrine. The former Northwest chef calls this chic custard concoction a "bread pudding." Pardon me—this is not bread pudding. Rather, it is a deep, dark, chocolate-fueled indulgence worthy of four-star status. Thank goodness the recipe, with its shamelessly rich brownie base, makes more than enough extra brownies to fill in the terrine.

Midway through the recipe, Karp's instructions are to cut the cooled brownies into 1-inch squares. Good idea—it makes snacking irresistible. So go ahead, indulge in a few bites, share a few others, then complete the recipe. When the midnight countdown begins and you're ready to serve, encircle it with ROSEMARY WHITE CHOCOLATE GANACHE (page 56), cap a slice with a scoop of vanilla ice cream, or leave it deliciously as is.

SERVES 14 TO 16

Start-the-New-Year-with-Chocolate Brownie Terrine

BROWNIES

1⅓ cups **cake flour**

¾ cup **unsweetened Dutch process cocoa powder**

¾ teaspoon **baking powder**

½ teaspoon **salt**

5 **eggs,** at room temperature

1 teaspoon **pure vanilla extract**

1½ cups plus 3 tablespoons **unsalted butter,** at room temperature

1¾ cups **granulated sugar**

continued

1. **TO MAKE THE BROWNIES:** Preheat the oven to 350°F. Lightly grease a 13-by-9-by-2-inch baking pan with cooking spray. To make the brownies easier to remove, line the pan lengthwise with a 17-by-8-inch sheet of parchment paper and use the overhang as handles. Lightly grease the parchment and set aside.

2. Into a medium bowl, sift together the flour, cocoa, baking powder, and salt, then lightly whisk. Break the eggs into a small bowl, and add the vanilla, but do not mix.

continued

Chocolate Brownie Terrine *continued*

CUSTARD

¾ cup **milk**

1 cup **heavy (whipping) cream**

¼ cup plus 2 tablespoons **granulated sugar**

8 ounces **high-quality bitter-sweet chocolate,** broken into small pieces

4 **eggs,** at room temperature

1 teaspoon **pure vanilla extract**

1 tablespoon **Cognac** (optional)

Powdered sugar for dusting

3. In a stand mixer set on low speed, beat the butter until creamy, about 30 seconds. On medium speed, beat in the sugar until light and fluffy. On low speed, add the flour mixture in 3 additions, alternating with the egg mixture in 2 additions until well blended, scraping down the sides and bottom of the bowl as necessary. Spread the batter into the prepared pan. Bake until the top springs back when lightly touched and a toothpick in the center comes out clean, about 30 minutes. Transfer to a rack to cool. Cut into 1-inch cubes. Leave the cubes out to dry, exposed to the air, for 6 to 8 hours or overnight.

4. TO MAKE THE CUSTARD: Preheat the oven to 325°F. Butter a 2-quart porcelain terrine mold, a bread pan, a soufflé dish, or any other container that catches your fancy. Prepare a water bath by placing a terry-cloth washcloth in the bottom of a roasting pan or similar-style pan, and place the terrine on top of it. (This prevents the dish from sliding, insulates the bottom of the terrine, and helps prevent overcooking.) Set aside.

5. In a saucepan over medium heat, bring the milk, cream, and sugar just to a simmer. Meanwhile, place the chocolate in a medium bowl. Pour the hot cream mixture over the chocolate. Let stand for 3 to 4 minutes, then whisk until smooth.

6. In a small bowl, whisk together the eggs, vanilla, and Cognac, if desired, then slowly whisk this mixture into the chocolate until just combined. Scrape any foam off the top and discard.

7. TO ASSEMBLE: Tightly arrange the brownie cubes in the prepared mold, leaving room at the top for the custard to cover them. Pour the custard over the brownies and let stand. Using a large spoon, poke and press the brownies to make sure they are well saturated. Add more custard, if necessary, to rise above the brownies (they'll absorb liquid as they bake).

8. Using oven mitts, pull out the middle oven shelf partway, and place the prepared roasting pan on it. Carefully pour enough hot water into the roasting pan to reach halfway up the sides of the terrine. Bake until an instant-read thermometer inserted in the middle reads 170°F, about 90 minutes. Check after 60 minutes, then keep checking intermittently. The finished terrine will be very firm. Cool to room temperature, then refrigerate until well chilled.

9. To remove the terrine, place the baking dish in a warm water bath for a few minutes, then invert it onto a cutting board or serving platter. Use a stencil or dust freely with powdered sugar. Allow the terrine to come to room temperature before slicing.

INDEX

A

Almonds
   La Galette des Rois, 114–15
   Jerusalem Olive Oil Cake with
      Orange Marmalade and
      Almonds, 57–59
   Petite French Almond Cakes with
      Champagne, 143–44
   Saint Lucia's Saffron Crown, 82–83
   Slivered Biscotti with Gelato
      Affogato, 148
   Triple-Treat Almond Bars, 152
The Amazing Leftover Eggnog and
   Cinnamon Roll Bread Pudding, 104
Apples
   Backyard Apple Tree Crisp, 43
   Bubbee and Me Baked Candy
      Apples, 62
   It's-Nighttime-and-They're-*Still*-
      Hungry Apple Pastry with
      Calvados and Golden Raisins, 31
   It's-Thanksgiving-Morning-but-
      They-*Still*-Deserve-Something-
      Special Apple Puff Pancake, 30–31
   Pear-Apple Strudel with
      Rosemary White Chocolate
      Ganache, 54–56
   Sweet Onion, Apple, and Cheese
      Tart, 106
Apricots
   Apricot Jam and Coconut
      Squares, 123
   Apricot Mustard, 108–9
   Apricot Nut Rugelach, 52–53
   Selma's Apricot Noodle Kugel, 64
Autumn's Best Crisscross Cookies,
   24

B

Backyard Apple Tree Crisp, 43
Baking sheets, 13
Baking tips, 10–17
Banana Wafer Pudding and Pie, 133–35
Biscotti, Slivered, with Gelato
   Affogato, 148
Biscuits, Soul-Satisfying, and Gravy,
   128–29
Blessed Be Breakfast Quiche, 25–26
Bloody Mary and Baked Mushroom
   Omelet, 155–56
Bloody Mary Sauce, 155
Blueberries
   Crunchy-Topped Blueberry
      Muffins, 28
   Jamberry Maple Syrup, 105
   Spiced Blueberry Sauce, 154
Boxing Day Scones with Warm
   Strawberry Jam, 103
Bread
   The Amazing Leftover Eggnog and
      Cinnamon Roll Bread Pudding,
      104
   The Kids' Cinnamon-Roll
      Christmas Tree, 84–85
   Mama's Yummy Sweet Spoonbread
      Soufflé, 130
   Saint Lucia's Saffron Crown, 82–83
   Soul-Satisfying Biscuits and
      Gravy, 128–29
   "Two Please" Thanksgiving Dinner
      Orange Rolls, 32–33
Brownie Terrine, Start-the-New-
   Year-with-Chocolate, 161–63
Brown Sugar Benne Cookies and
   North African Mint Tea, 121–22
Bubbee and Me Baked Candy Apples, 62
Buckingham Palace Shortbread, 100
Butter, 11

C

Cake pans, 13–14
Cakes. *See also* Cupcakes
   Church Supper Carrot Cake with
      Pineapple and Walnuts, 137
   Church Supper Carrot Cake with
      Two Frostings, 136–37
   La Galette des Rois, 114–15
   Jerusalem Olive Oil Cake with
      Orange Marmalade and
      Almonds, 57–59
   "Let's Make a Dreidel" Chocolate
      Cake, 68–69
   A Nice Little Cheesecake, 66–67
   Petite French Almond Cakes with
      Champagne, 143–44
   "Shall I Be Mother?" Teatime
      Pound Cake, 112–13
   Snowflake Cake, 93–97
   Sticky-Top Gingerbread, 41
   Stir-Up Sunday Fruitcake, 80–81
   storing, 16–17
   Streusel-Top Sour Cream Coffee
      Cake, 60
   The Ultimate Dinner Guest's
      Gingerbread, 40–41
Candied Pecans, 131
Candy Cane Cupcakes, 97
Cardamom Custard Sauce, 39
Cardamom Pistachio Rugelach, 52–53
Carrots
   Church Supper Carrot Cake with
      Pineapple and Walnuts, 137
   Church Supper Carrot Cake with
      Two Frostings, 136–37
Cashew Caramel Cracker Bars,
   125–26
Cheese. *See also* Cream cheese
   Blessed Be Breakfast Quiche,
      25–26
   Bloody Mary and Baked Mushroom
      Omelet, 155–56
   Chip-Shot Pizza with Black Forest
      Ham, Smoked Gouda, and
      Apricot Mustard, 108–9
   Flashy Cocktail Rings with a Trio
      of Seeds, 89
   Golden Savory Cheese Coins,
      65
   Gruyère Horseradish Popovers,
      88
   New Year's Eve Meringue Roulade,
      157–59
   Stilton Pinwheels with Walnuts
      and Honey, 111
   Sweet Onion, Apple, and Cheese
      Tart, 106
Cherry, Dried, and Wild Rice Muffins,
   127
Chip-Shot Pizza with Black Forest
   Ham, Smoked Gouda, and Apricot
   Mustard, 108–9
Chocolate
   Cashew Caramel Cracker Bars,
      125–26
   Chocolate Almond Cinnamon
      Stars, 51
   Chocolate Chip Gingerbread
      Cupcakes, 41
   Chocolate Gelt Hide-a-Cookies,
      48–51
   Chocolate Peanut Butter Surprise
      Cupcakes, 138–39
   Hot Chocolate Popovers, 88
   "Let's Make a Dreidel" Chocolate
      Cake, 68–69
   Midnight Cowboy Chocolate Chip
      Cookies, 145
   Stained Glass Candy Cookie
      Charms, 75

Start-the-New-Year-with-Chocolate Brownie Terrine, 161–63
Triple-Treat Almond Bars, 152
Triple-Treat Touchdown Bars, 151–52
Christmas Day Trifles for You and Me, 90–92
Church Lady's Frosting, 137
Church Supper Carrot Cake with Pineapple and Walnuts, 137
Church Supper Carrot Cake with Two Frostings, 136 37
Coconut
    Apricot Jam and Coconut Squares, 123
    Church Lady's Frosting, 137
    Midnight Cowboy Chocolate Chip Cookies, 145
Cookies
    Apricot Jam and Coconut Squares, 123
    Apricot Nut Rugelach, 52–53
    Autumn's Best Crisscross Cookies, 24
    Brown Sugar Benne Cookies and North African Mint Tea, 121–22
    Buckingham Palace Shortbread, 100
    Cardamom Pistachio Rugelach, 52–53
    Cashew Caramel Cracker Bars, 125–26
    Chocolate Almond Cinnamon Stars, 51
    Chocolate Gelt Hide-a-Cookies, 48–51
    Crunchy Nut Caramel Bars, 126
    Cut-Out Ginger Gobblers, 20–21
    Gingerbread Men and a Few of Their Holiday Friends, 73–74
    Golden Raisin Crisscross Cookies, 24

Hanukkah Frosted Cookie Cutouts, 46–47
Kwanzaa Puzzle Cookies, 118–20
Linzer Wreaths, 77–78
mailing, 16
Midnight Cowboy Chocolate Chip Cookies, 145
Misbehavin' Girls Peanut Butter Cookie Sandwiches, 120
Next Year's Fortune Cookies, 146
Old-as-Pilgrims Molasses Crinkles, 22–23
Razzle-Dazzle Dreidels, 47
Retro Raisin Crisscross Cookies, 24
Rugelach with Marmalade, Sage, and Pine Nuts, 53
Slivered Biscotti with Gelato Affogato, 148
Sofia's Snow Pillows, 79
Stained Glass Candy Cookie Charms, 75
storing, 16
Sweet Pumpkin and Sesame Seed Cookies, 122
Triple-Treat Almond Bars, 152
Triple-Treat Touchdown Bars, 151–52
Victorian Scrap Cookies, 76
Walnut Walkaways, 149–50
Crackers
    Cashew Caramel Cracker Bars, 125–26
    Crunchy Nut Caramel Bars, 126
    Flashy Cocktail Rings with a Trio of Seeds, 89
    Golden Savory Cheese Coins, 65
Cranberries
    Jamberry Maple Syrup, 105
Cream, 13

Cream cheese
    Apricot Nut Rugelach, 52–53
    Cardamom Pistachio Rugelach, 52–53
    Chocolate Peanut Butter Surprise Cupcakes, 138–39
    Church Lady's Frosting, 137
    Cream Cheese Frosting, 137
    A Nice Little Cheesecake, 66–67
    Rugelach with Marmalade, Sage, and Pine Nuts, 53
    Selma's Apricot Noodle Kugel, 64
    Walnut Walkaways, 149–50
Crisp, Backyard Apple Tree, 43
Crunchy Nut Caramel Bars, 126
Crunchy-Topped Blueberry Muffins, 28
Crust, Flaky Pastry, 25
Cupcakes
    Candy Cane Cupcakes, 97
    Chocolate Chip Gingerbread Cupcakes, 41
    Chocolate Peanut Butter Surprise Cupcakes, 138–39
Cut-Out Ginger Gobblers, 20–21

D
Dutch Baby Pancake, 153

E
Eggnog and Cinnamon Roll Bread Pudding, The Amazing Leftover, 104
Eggs, 12
    Bloody Mary and Baked Mushroom Omelet, 155–56
    Mama's Yummy Sweet Spoonbread Soufflé, 130
Erna Neuman's Icing, 47

F
Flaky Pastry Crust, 25
Flashy Cocktail Rings with a Trio of Seeds, 89
Flour, 11–12
Fortune Cookies, Next Year's, 146
Frostings, icings, and glazes
    Church Lady's Frosting, 137
    Cream Cheese Frosting, 137
    Erna Neuman's Icing, 47
    Grandmother's Grown-Up Glaze, 23
Fruit, dried. See also individual fruits
    Autumn's Best Crisscross Cookies, 24
    Rustic Dried Fruit Tart, 37–38
    Stir-Up Sunday Fruitcake, 80–81

G
La Galette des Rois, 114–15
Ganache, Rosemary White Chocolate, 56
Gelato Affogato, 148
Gingerbread
    Chocolate Chip Gingerbread Cupcakes, 41
    Gingerbread Men and a Few of Their Holiday Friends, 73–74
    Sticky-Top Gingerbread, 41
    The Ultimate Dinner Guest's Gingerbread, 40–41
    Victorian Scrap Cookies, 76
Glazes. See Frostings, icings, and glazes
Golden Raisin Crisscross Cookies, 24
Golden Savory Cheese Coins, 65
Grandmother's Grown-Up Glaze, 23
Gravy, Soul-Satisfying Biscuits and, 128–29
Gruyère Horseradish Popovers, 88

H

Ham, Black Forest, Chip-Shot Pizza with Smoked Gouda, Apricot Mustard, and, 108–9

Hanukkah Frosted Cookie Cutouts, 46–47

Hazelnuts
Linzer Wreaths, 77–78
Pear-Apple Strudel with Rosemary White Chocolate Ganache, 54–56

Hot Chocolate Popovers, 88

I

Ice cream
Gelato Affogato, 148

Icings. *See* Frostings, icings, and glazes

It's-Nighttime-and-They're-*Still*-Hungry Apple Pastry with Calvados and Golden Raisins, 31

It's-Thanksgiving-Morning-but-They-*Still* Deserve Something-Special Apple Puff Pancake, 30–31

J

Jamberry Maple Syrup, 105

Jams, preserves, and marmalades
Apricot Jam and Coconut Squares, 123
Boxing Day Scones with Warm Strawberry Jam, 103
Christmas Day Trifles for You and Me, 90–92
Jerusalem Olive Oil Cake with Orange Marmalade and Almonds, 57–59
Linzer Wreaths, 77–78
Rugelach with Marmalade, Sage, and Pine Nuts, 53

Jerusalem Olive Oil Cake with Orange Marmalade and Almonds, 57–59

K

Kids, baking with, 17

The Kids' Cinnamon-Roll Christmas Tree, 84–85

Kugel, Selma's Apricot Noodle, 64

Kwanzaa Puzzle Cookies, 118–20

L

"Let's Make a Dreidel" Chocolate Cake, 68–69

Linzer Wreaths, 77–78

M

Mama's Yummy Sweet Spoonbread Soufflé, 130

Maple Syrup, Jamberry, 105

Margarine, 11

Measuring cups and spoons, 13

Midnight Cowboy Chocolate Chip Cookies, 145

Milk, 12–13

Misbehavin' Girls Peanut Butter Cookie Sandwiches, 120

Muffins
Crunchy-Topped Blueberry Muffins, 28
Wild Rice and Dried Cherry Muffins, 127

Mushroom Omelet, Baked, Bloody Mary and, 155–56

Mustard, Apricot, 108–9

N

New Year's Eve Meringue Roulade, 157–59

Next Year's Fortune Cookies, 146

A Nice Little Cheesecake, 66–67

Noodle Kugel, Selma's Apricot, 64

North African Mint Tea, 122

Nuts. *See also individual nuts*
Apricot Nut Rugelach, 52–53
Crunchy Nut Caramel Bars, 126
Stir-Up Sunday Fruitcake, 80–81

O

Old-as-Pilgrims Molasses Crinkles, 22–23

Olive Oil Cake, Jerusalem, with Orange Marmalade and Almonds, 57–59

Omelet, Bloody Mary and Baked Mushroom, 155–56

Onion, Apple, and Cheese Tart, Sweet, 106

Orange Morning Relish, Strawberry, 154

P

Pancakes
Dutch Baby Pancake, 153
It's-Thanksgiving-Morning-but-They-*Still*-Deserve-Something-Special Apple Puff Pancake, 30–31

Pastry Cream, 90

Peanut butter
Chocolate Peanut Butter Surprise Cupcakes, 138–39
Kwanzaa Puzzle Cookies, 118–20
Midnight Cowboy Chocolate Chip Cookies, 145
Misbehavin' Girls Peanut Butter Cookie Sandwiches, 120

Pear-Apple Strudel with Rosemary White Chocolate Ganache, 54–56

Pecans
Apricot Jam and Coconut Squares, 123
Apricot Nut Rugelach, 52–53
Candied Pecans, 131
Midnight Cowboy Chocolate Chip Cookies, 145
Selma's Apricot Noodle Kugel, 64
Sofia's Snow Pillows, 79
Southern Comfort Sweet Potato Pecan Pie, 131–32
Streusel-Top Sour Cream Coffee Cake, 60

Petite French Almond Cakes with Champagne, 143–44

Phyllo pastry
Pear-Apple Strudel with Rosemary White Chocolate Ganache, 54–56

Pies
Banana Wafer Pudding and Pie, 133–35
Southern Comfort Sweet Potato Pecan Pie, 131–32
storing, 17
Vida Lee's Maple Pumpkin Pie, 35–36

Pineapple, Church Supper Carrot Cake with Walnuts and, 137

Pinwheels, Stilton, with Walnuts and Honey, 111

Pistachio Rugelach, Cardamom, 52–53

Pizza, Chip-Shot, with Black Forest Ham, Smoked Gouda, and Apricot Mustard, 108–9

Popovers
Gruyère Horseradish Popovers, 88
Hot Chocolate Popovers, 88
Without Thinking Twice Perfect Popovers, 87–88

Puddings
    The Amazing Leftover Eggnog and
        Cinnamon Roll Bread Pudding,
        104
    Banana Wafer Pudding and Pie,
        133–35
Puff pastry
    La Galette des Rois, 114–15
    Stilton Pinwheels with Walnuts
        and Honey, 111
Pumpkin Pie, Vida Lee's Maple,
    35–36
Pumpkin Seed Cookies, Sweet
    Sesame and, 122

Q

Quiche, Blessed Be Breakfast, 25–26

R

Raisins
    Apricot Nut Rugelach, 52–53
    Cardamom Pistachio Rugelach,
        52–53
    Golden Raisin Crisscross Cookies,
        24
    It's-Nighttime-and-They're-*Still*-
        Hungry Apple Pastry with
        Calvados and Golden Raisins, 31
    Retro Raisin Crisscross Cookies, 24
    Saint Lucia's Saffron Crown, 82–83
    Stir-Up Sunday Fruitcake, 80–81
Razzle-Dazzle Dreidels, 47
Retro Raisin Crisscross Cookies, 24
Rolls
    The Amazing Leftover Eggnog and
        Cinnamon Roll Bread Pudding, 104
    The Kids' Cinnamon-Roll
        Christmas Tree, 84–85
    "Two Please" Thanksgiving Dinner
        Orange Rolls, 32–33

Rosemary White Chocolate Ganache,
    56
Rugelach
    Apricot Nut Rugelach, 52–53
    Cardamom Pistachio Rugelach,
        52–53
    Rugelach with Marmalade, Sage,
        and Pine Nuts, 53
Rustic Dried Fruit Tart, 37–38

S

Saint Lucia's Saffron Crown, 82–83
Salt, 12
Sauces
    Bloody Mary Sauce, 155
    Cardamom Custard Sauce, 39
    Rosemary White Chocolate
        Ganache, 56
    Spiced Blueberry Sauce, 154
    Strawberry Orange Morning
        Relish, 154
Sausage
    Soul-Satisfying Biscuits and
        Gravy, 128–29
Scones, Boxing Day, with Warm
    Strawberry Jam, 103
Selma's Apricot Noodle Kugel, 64
Sesame seeds
    Brown Sugar Benne Cookies and
        North African Mint Tea, 121–22
    Sweet Pumpkin and Sesame Seed
        Cookies, 122
    toasting, 122
"Shall I Be Mother?" Teatime Pound
    Cake, 112–13
Shortbread, Buckingham Palace, 100
Shortening, 11
Slivered Biscotti with Gelato
    Affogato, 148
Snowflake Cake, 93–95

Sofia's Snow Pillows, 79
Soufflé, Mama's Yummy Sweet
    Spoonbread, 130
Soul-Satisfying Biscuits and Gravy,
    128–29
Southern Comfort Sweet Potato
    Pecan Pie, 131–32
Spiced Blueberry Sauce, 154
Spoonbread Soufflé, Mama's Yummy
    Sweet, 130
Stained Glass Candy Cookie Charms, 75
Start-the-New-Year-with-Chocolate
    Brownie Terrine, 161–63
Sticky-Top Gingerbread, 41
Stilton Pinwheels with Walnuts and
    Honey, 111
Stir-Up Sunday Fruitcake, 80–81
Storage tips, 16–17
Strawberry Orange Morning Relish,
    154
Streusel-Top Sour Cream Coffee
    Cake, 60
Strudel, Pear-Apple, with Rosemary
    White Chocolate Ganache, 54–56
Sugar, 12
Sweet Onion, Apple, and Cheese
    Tart, 106
Sweet Potato Pecan Pie, Southern
    Comfort, 131–32
Sweet Pumpkin and Sesame Seed
    Cookies, 122

T

Tarts
    Rustic Dried Fruit Tart, 37–38
    Sweet Onion, Apple, and Cheese
        Tart, 106
Tea, North African Mint, 122
Terrine, Start-the-New-Year-with-
    Chocolate Brownie, 161–63

Tomatoes
    Bloody Mary Sauce, 155
Tools, 14–15
Trifles, Christmas Day, for You and
    Me, 90–92
Triple-Treat Almond Bars, 152
Triple-Treat Touchdown Bars,
    151–52
"Two Please" Thanksgiving Dinner
    Orange Rolls, 32–33

U

The Ultimate Dinner Guest's
    Gingerbread, 40–41

V

Victorian Scrap Cookies, 76
Vida Lee's Maple Pumpkin Pie,
    35–36

W

Walnuts
    Apricot Nut Rugelach, 52–53
    Church Supper Carrot Cake with
        Pineapple and Walnuts, 137
    The Kids' Cinnamon-Roll
        Christmas Tree, 84–85
    Stilton Pinwheels with Walnuts
        and Honey, 111
    Streusel-Top Sour Cream Coffee
        Cake, 60
Walnut Walkaways, 149–50
White chocolate
    Rosemary White Chocolate
        Ganache, 56
    Snowflake Cake, 93–97
Wild Rice and Dried Cherry Muffins,
    127
Without Thinking Twice Perfect
    Popovers, 87–88

TABLE OF EQUIVALENTS

The exact equivalents in the following tables have been rounded for convenience.

LIQUID / DRY MEASURES

U.S.	METRIC
¼ teaspoon	1.25 milliliters
½ teaspoon	2.5 milliliters
1 teaspoon	5 milliliters
1 tablespoon (3 teaspoons)	15 milliliters
1 fluid ounce (2 tablespoons)	30 milliliters
¼ cup	60 milliliters
⅓ cup	80 milliliters
½ cup	120 milliliters
1 cup	240 milliliters
1 pint (2 cups)	480 milliliters
1 quart (4 cups, 32 ounces)	960 milliliters
1 gallon (4 quarts)	3.84 liters
1 ounce (by weight)	28 grams
1 pound	454 grams
2.2 pounds	1 kilogram

OVEN TEMPERATURE

FAHRENHEIT	CELSIUS	GAS
250	120	½
275	140	1
300	150	2
325	160	3
350	180	4
375	190	5
400	200	6
425	220	7
450	230	8
475	240	9
500	260	10

LENGTH

U.S.	METRIC
⅛ inch	3 millimeters
¼ inch	6 millimeters
½ inch	12 millimeters
1 inch	2.5 centimeters